Moscow Masala

Dr. Mandar V. Bichu

Popular Prakashan
www.popularprakashan.com

Published by
Harsha Bhatkal for
POPULAR PRAKASHAN PVT. LTD.
301, Mahalaxmi Chambers
22, Bhulabhai Desai Road
Mumbai - 400 026

First Published 2013

(4367)
ISBN: 978-81-7991-808-1

Disclaimer -
This book is a work of fiction. Names of some real places, institutions and people have been used to aid the story-telling. There is no intention to imply otherwise.

Cover Design: Gaman Palem
Typesetter: Mahendra Ghanekar

PRINTED IN INDIA
by Sai Print 'o' Pack
New Delhi - 110 020

Contents

Dedicated to my dear friend
Dr Bharat Kaushik,
through whose eyes
I saw Russia!

Prologue

It was pitch dark inside. I couldn't see anything. Of course, when your head is forcibly pushed into a jute-bag, you can't really see anything. The suffocation was unbearable. I was gradually losing consciousness, but even in that dazed state of mind, I could feel the weight and pain of every blow to my head.

Thud...thud...thud...thud.... It wouldn't be long now. A few more blows and my head would split into pieces.

I woke up with a violent start. It was 4.30 am. To my relief I found my head resting on the pillow and quite intact. Just that it was heavy from the hangover and clammy from sweat. I could still hear the loud thuds.

The noise was coming from downstairs. No, it was not just a nightmare; somebody was really banging hard on the main door as if in a bid to tear it down.

Who could it be at this unearthly hour? Wasn't it Sunday?

Nervously I pulled myself out of my warm and cosy bed and scrambled downstairs. Through the foggy eyehole, I could see 4-5 faces--all heavily hooded and peering intently at my door.

My heart missed a beat. My brain froze with fear. What was happening? What was wrong?

"Open the door immediately. Police."

I hesitantly opened the door. Without any warning, the first person grabbed me by the throat; the second handcuffed me and the rest just stood around looking menacingly at me. One thing was slightly reassuring though--they were real policemen and not some goons.

The officer walked in. The glint in his eyes was unmistakable. Looking me square in the eyes, he asked, "Where is the dead body?"

I looked at him blankly.

"D-d-dead body? I don't know what you are talking about? Officer, there seems to be some misunderstanding."

The stinging slap on my face told me that he clearly was in no mood to listen to me!

He barked orders to his team.

"Go and check the apartment. I want to nail this bastard!"

By then I had resigned myself to fate. I just kept looking at the policemen, busy turning my place upside down.

After half an hour of intensive search, they reported back to the officer.

"Sir, there is nothing in the house."

He looked at me with contempt and said, "Okay, haul him into the van. Let's take him in. He will talk. They all do!"

✣

It had been more than an hour since they had brought me to the police station. I was locked up in a big room, which was empty save a small table and two chairs at the centre. The single dim tubelight made the old, grey walls look older and even greyer than they actually were. One of the walls had a large mirror. Even though it looked like any other mirror, I was sure that it was a mirror-finished glass and there were people behind that, closely observing me. I had seen enough Hollywood crime thrillers to know that.

After walking about aimlessly for almost half an hour, I sat down at one of the chairs and tried hard to make sense of the situation, but for the life of me I could not fathom what was happening. Why was I there? What dead body were they talking about? Whose dead body? What the hell was happening?

Just then the door opened. A tall, hefty guy, wearing a brown overcoat, walked in. He had a pronounced limp. Pulling up the chair across the table, he positioned himself opposite to me.

The authority on his face clearly revealed his position as some senior official. But he also looked nervous and disheveled. His face was puffy. His eyes were bloodshot. For five minutes he just sat there smoking a cigar and looking at me intently.

Then he asked me in a deep baritone. "Tell me all about yourself. Right from the time you decided to come to Russia. What made you come to Russia? What are you doing here? Everything."

All about myself! From the time I came to Russia! I did not know where to start. So much had transpired. How the hell was I going to tell him all that? But I had no choice. I started to talk.

"My name is Sadanand Borkar...."

FLASHBACK

Stamped for life?

June 10, 1983

I reached college at 10 o'clock in the morning. The college corridor was milling with students.

"Hey, I passed."

"Thank God, it's finally over."

"How much did you get in PCB? And in PCM?"

It was the day of my standard XII results--from every direction came the typical post-result exchanges. Shouts, laughter, back-slapping--there was so much noise all around. The atmosphere was one of euphoria and excitement.

As I walked towards the notice board, I caught a glimpse of my best friend. He was busy discussing his marks with another classmate. I thought of stopping to check how he had fared...but moved on to check my own marks first. For a fleeting moment, I felt as if he was deliberately avoiding me. Why on earth would he do that?

Suddenly my knees began to feel weak. My stomach felt like a tightly coiled knot in a hollow pit. It seemed as if the deafening noise around me had dissolved into deathly silence. As I worked my way through the crowd to get to the notice board, I got the feeling that my batchmates were making way for me by deliberately turning away. I began to feel nauseous. Locating my number was a hard task, made even more difficult by the foggy glass cover. And then I finally found it!

It was the third last number in the first column. 151065. It was badly printed. But the letters against the number were very clear--'FAIL'.

The suspense was finally over. The nausea subsided. My stomach loosened up. A peculiar sense of calm descended on my jangled nerves. I quietly turned around and headed towards the office to collect my marksheet.

As I came out of the office, a group of well-wishers and friends gathered around me. Everyone was trying his best to console and offer encouragement.

"Where did it go wrong?" someone asked me.

Without saying a word, I just showed him my marksheet.

'English-60, Marathi-62, Physics-70, Chemistry-67, Biology-66, Maths-5!'

It was an all-out massacre. Maths-5!

For a moment, he was too shocked to say anything! To his credit, he somehow found his tongue.

"It must be a printing mistake. I am sure it is. Give it for re-evaluation. Remember last year... Naresh's marks were all botched up while printing. I am sure your case is similar."

The dear soul was trying so hard to sound sympathetic. I smiled weakly and nodded though I was absolutely sure that my case was nothing like Naresh's. In fact I did not even know who this Naresh was! The only thing I knew for sure is that I had neither any reason nor any inclination to go for re-evaluation!

I quietly admitted to myself that those marks seemed to be a fair reflection of my performance. How I had hated Maths; how I had left so many questions unanswered in all my papers; how I had messed up my preparations; how I had not wanted to appear for my exams that year....

As the crowd finally dispersed, I stood alone in the empty corridor. I saw a peon closing the office doors. I had hardly spoken a word after seeing my marksheet. Suddenly I got an inexplicable urge to speak to him.

I called out, "Psst...boss!"

He looked at me with concern and asked, "Yes, what happened? Passed?"

I clammed up. Dumbly shaking my head, I waved him goodbye and started walking away.

Walking towards the railway station, I wondered how I was going to break the news at home. Strangely, I did not feel anything inside me--no sadness, no anxiety, no anger, no 'why me'... just an all-engulfing numbness.

As the train began to move, I remembered the year gone by. The year that was going to decide my future; the year that was going to give me a chance to become a doctor; and the year that had now stamped a big fat 'F' against my name! How could that happen? How could I have let it happen? Innumerable questions buzzed in my head.... Somewhere along the way, I dozed off.

"O bhaau, yeh aakhri station hai!"

I woke up with a start. The road from station to home seemed unending. Step-by-step, following my long shadow, I finally reached my house. The door opened almost as soon as I rang the bell. My father, mother, sister looked expectantly at me. I didn't say anything--just thrust the marksheet in my father's hand.

Standing there, I kept waiting for my father's standard tirade to begin. I wanted him to shout at me; I wanted him to slap me; I wanted him to say, "I told you so." But he did not do anything of the sort. He just came and hugged me tightly!

He kept repeating, "Don't worry my son. This is not the end of the world. There will be more opportunities." He seemed to be consoling and convincing himself rather than me. Shoulders drooping, eyes glistening, voice breaking--he suddenly looked much older than he was.

Something churned inside me. The enormity of my loss was finally sinking in. I felt ashamed; I felt guilty; I felt exposed. The numbness disappeared and an overwhelming feeling of sadness hit me like a wave. The throat hurt; the eyes smarted.

For a while I desperately tried to control my feelings. Then I simply gave up. I did something that I had not done in many years. I cried... I cried inconsolably! It was the lowest point of my life so far!

□□□

Charting a new course

June 15, 1985

Again I had come home late. It was almost midnight. Bloody Kasara train! Had to get delayed every single day! As I stepped in, I saw my father glaring angrily at me. Mother and sister were cowering behind him; waiting anxiously to see what would happen next. As expected, my father flew off the handle. Once again I would have to hear his oft-repeated sermon, one of his favourites.

"You failed in standard XII, I did not say anything. I said mistakes do happen. I provided you with the best tuitions. But then what did you do the next year? You got average marks and once again fluffed your chances to study medicine. I still said nothing. Then out of the blue, you decided to join that new pharmacy college in Pune. Did I stop you from doing that? No. Do you have any idea how much I am paying as your college and hostel fees? Now you are telling me that the college is not good; the professors cannot even speak English properly; the labs are not well-equipped! For the last two months, whenever you come home on weekends, you hardly ever reach home before midnight. What are you doing till so late in the night? What exactly do you intend to do with your life? Can you at least spell that out for me? I am really sick and tired of your wayward ways. Are you simply going to waste your life and all my money?"

Standing before him, I quietly weighed my options. Should I tell him now or later? How will he take it? Suddenly something came over me. To hell with it! Why should I keep it under wraps? It is my life, anyway.

I tried to speak confidently but I could only manage a croak. "Dad, I am not completing the pharmacy course. I have decided to drop out."

The statement had an instant impact. My family stood transfixed. They looked at me, dumbstruck.

My father was flummoxed. "W-What?"

I continued, "Yes, dad. I have now decided to go to Russia. My friend, Vijay, has given me all the information. The Russian government is inviting applications for medical courses. It is an all-expenses-paid course."

Father looked like he was going to have an apoplectic fit any moment. He burst out, "Are you out of your mind? Do you even know what you are saying? Russia! Have you heard anything sillier? US, UK, Canada–yes, people go there to study. Not to Russia. They cannot even speak English there!"

The cat was out of the bag! My voice was calm and confident now. "I know dad, they speak Russian there! These last two months I have been coming home late just because I am taking weekend courses in Russian. Coming from Pune, I go to Peddar Road to attend Russian language classes at the House of Soviet Cultural Centre. Next month, I have my assessments. I am sure I will do well."

There was a sullen silence in the room. Nobody had anything to say to me and I had already said my piece!

□□□

Preparations

After my dramatic declaration, things had turned really sour at home. After a week, I added more fuel to the fire by leaving my Pune hostel for good! Now the battlelines were officially drawn. I was the outcast. My father stopped talking to me. My mother also preferred to keep quiet because she was so apprehensive of offending either of us. My only solace was my sister but she too preferred to stay silent in front of dad.

Staying at home now became problematic. To avoid further confrontation, I would get out of my room only after my father had left for work. I would somehow while away my time till evening, when I would leave for my night classes. Coping with the tension was getting increasingly difficult. The gloomy atmosphere at home was taking a toll on all of us.

Then one day, sorry, one night a miracle happened!

It was well past 11 pm. Once again, I was coming back late from my night classes. I rang the bell, fully prepared to run into my raging father. Mom opened the door. She was smiling. I was surprised to see her smile after such a long time!

I warily asked, "What's the matter? Why are you smiling?"

Without saying anything, my mother just disappeared into the kitchen. I headed to my room, feeling jittery about what to expect. As I entered my room, I found my sister there. She too was smiling from ear to ear. Irritated, I barked, "What the heck? Would somebody care to tell me what's happening?"

But before I could go any further, she chirped, "Congrats, father has agreed to support your Russia plan!"

I looked at her uncomprehendingly. How could this have happened?

"Yes, your father has agreed to send you to Russia...because I have told him it is okay to send you there!" My Grandpa's booming voice came from behind.

"Grandpa, you..." Bewildered, I could just greet him with a shell-shocked expression.

Grandpa decided to show off. "Why are you looking like that? Don't you believe that your father always listens to his father?"

Dad was standing behind grandpa, looking like a sheepish schoolboy.

Grandpa continued, "Yes, I went and checked the place where you learn Russian. I even met your teacher. What's his name? Yes, Alexy. He told me that you are doing very well in the subject. He also told me how these professional courses are run by the Russian government to pick up talented students from all over the world."

Suddenly father decided to enter the conversation in his typical action-plan kind of way. "Okay, you go to sleep now. Tomorrow morning, be ready at eight sharp. Your grandpa is taking us to meet a friend."

Still very confused, I looked at him searchingly. He had a goofy smile on his face!

I did not want to spoil the good mood by asking too many questions. So, I decided to simply shut up and wait!

✣

"What exactly are we doing here, Grandpa? Who is this friend of yours? And what is he going to do?" I finally gathered courage to ask the questions that had been bothering me since the previous night. It was almost 2 pm and we were still waiting for 'Grandpa's friend', whose identity he refused to reveal. He just glared me into silence.

A two-hour local train journey had brought us to VT station. We had walked around for about 45 minutes down winding gullies before finding this dilapidated building that looked like a relic from the colonial era. Since then more than two hours had passed sitting in the creaking, bug-infested chairs at the dusty, musty reception area of the dingy office.

At 2:15 pm a man, well over 70, walked in. There were around 10 men following him--each trying to tell him something, each trying to grab his attention. Tall, gaunt, unsmiling, wearing black-rimmed spectacles, loose-fitting khaki trousers and a baggy white shirt...the man looked vaguely familiar. Just as he was about to enter his office, he spotted the three of us. As his eyes fell on my grandfather, he stopped in his tracks.

"*Arre* Ramanand, what a surprise! It must be what...50 years since we last met?"

My grandpa stood up and hugged him tightly. "Kanna, you haven't forgotten?"

I could see tears welling in both men's eyes!

Then my grandfather turned to me and said, "This is the answer to all your queries. He is Mr Achyut Kannan, my classmate from Mangalore and the president of one of the biggest trade unions in India!"

Yes, that was it. I had seen him in the newspapers. He was one of the biggest Left leaders in India. Grandpa had really done his groundwork well!

✣

"What work brings you here Rama?"

Mr Kannan immediately came to the point. Even in his nostalgia, he was clear in his head. No old friend comes after 50 years to merely sit and chat about dead college professors and long lost girlfriends! There was work to be done and he wanted to know what!

Grandpa gave him a quick summary of my plans to go to Russia, with father adding a few details.

"So, you need my recommendation letter, huh? No problem. *Arre* Tukaram, please take out that recommendation letter *pro forma*. It is in that third file in the top drawer...not the one for Indian medical colleges, the one for Russian medical colleges."

So that was that. The veteran leader handed me his signed recommendation letter even before our cutting-*chai* arrived.

Only then the two old men chatted about the good old days and how sorely they missed them! When we finally came out of that building, our faces were beaming! Mission Russia was going somewhere!

□□□

Admission letter

August 25, 1985

Father arrived home with a furrowed forehead. My heart skipped a beat. This was his usual expression before launching into a tirade...and it was usually directed towards me! My hunch was spot-on!

"Sada, hasn't it been four weeks since you passed that Russian exam and we sent your application along with Mr Kannan's recommendation? They had told us that within three weeks they would be sending the confirmation letter. I have been regularly checking our letter box and even making rounds at the post-office but there is no news yet. What is the matter? Have you gone and checked the status of your application at the Russian Consulate?"

He looked worried. I was worried too but this was not the time to voice it. I said, "Don't worry, Dad. I had gone to the consulate two days back. They said that all the applications are approved only in Moscow and all the papers have been sent there."

As usual Dad was quick to point out the flaw in my reasoning. "But you had said that two of your friends have already got their admission letters. How did that happen? Didn't they appear for their test along with you?"

I had no answer. Actually the same question had been bothering me for sometime. How was it that they had got the letters and I had not? Had I been rejected for some silly reason? After all, who knew how the Russians went about their selection process! Was this going to be yet another false lead in my career?

"Have you written the return address properly on your application?" Dad's back-end enquiries began. God, there was no respite!

"Obviously Dad!"

Then it hit me. I stuttered. "Oh heck! Oh, no!"

"What are you saying?" He demanded an immediate explanation.

I stuttered again. "D-d-dad, I think...I think I may have messed up the return address."

Father could barely control his anger. Gritting his teeth, he asked, "And what exactly do you mean by 'messed up'?"

Nervously, I said, "I have given them the address of our new house in Mulund."

He looked at me, speechless. For once, he just did not know what to say!

When I had filled up the application form, we were to move into our new flat in Mulund within a fortnight. But some last minute technical hitches had delayed our shifting and we had stayed put in our old flat in Kalyan! Now, thanks to this confusion, there was a high probability that my admission letter had been delivered to my Mulund address!

Dad came over and gripped my arm and said, "Come, let us go to Mulund right now!"

✣

The building complex was still quite new. Only a few people had started living there. Their curious eyes closely followed our every movement as we reached our flat. Edgy, my father was unlike his usual efficient self and fumbled with the keys before finding the correct one. As he opened the door, I looked inside expectantly.

There it was! A long, yellow envelope was lying on the dusty floor. The stamped date told us that it had been lying there for more than a week. I opened it anxiously.

"Mr Sadanand Borkar, you have been selected as one of the candidates for the USSR's medical education program for foreign

students. You are requested to join the program from the second week of September, 1985. The final procedures will take place in the first week of September in Delhi, from where you will be departing to Moscow."

A huge wave of relief washed over me. As he wiped his moist eyes, my father allowed himself the rare luxury of a broad smile. He fondly patted my back and said, "Good job, my son. Finally you've done it!"

□□□

Chalo Delhi!

September 3, 1985

"It is high time we boarded the train, man!"

Kevin D'Souza literally shouted in my ear. I looked at my watch. Yes, it was indeed high time we boarded the train. Rajdhani Express was going to leave for Delhi in another five minutes.

When I had first arrived at Mumbai Central, I had had no idea that it was going be such a grand affair. But as it transpired, there were at least 80 people there to bid us, and our accompanying worried fathers, farewell. We were scheduled to leave for the USSR right after finishing the formalities in Delhi. Mothers, brothers, sisters, uncles, aunts, friends, and neighbours...all near and dear ones were there to see us (read Parag Shah, Yatin Patil, Nilesh Badrinath, Kevin D'Souza and me) off as we set out on our Russian adventure. So, here we were getting an intensely emotional (and immensely embarrassing!) send-off to Delhi. It was quite a scene!

Right there on the platform, an *aarti* was performed. All of us 'Russia-bound heroes' were garlanded and *kumkum tilaks* were put on our foreheads. Every well-wisher had something or the other to say to us and since we hardly had anything to say, we just kept nodding and smiling at everyone.

After all those 'Best wishes', 'Forget-me-not's, last minute suggestions, tight embraces, wan smiles and teary eyes, I almost felt like a parting newly-wed bride, leaving behind the past and entering an unknown future! The mental state of my colleagues was no different!

In the company of our fathers, when we five finally boarded the train, we all were wiping our tears unashamedly. As expected, the Rajdhani Express started dot on time!

September 4, 1985

In Delhi, we assembled at the Russian Embassy hall. Around 150 students from various parts of India were already waiting there expectantly.

Chatting up with other students, we came to know something else...that perhaps our single-minded efforts to learn Russian had been rather a waste of time! Most of those 'selections' (sorry, '*Selecsons*'!) had hardly bothered to learn Russian, instead they had focused on something else altogether–on getting heavyweight recommendations from Indian political leaders!

"I am Vladimir Gromyko, the Senior Attache at the embassy."

The noise in the hall immediately subsided as a bald, corpulent, middle-aged Russian bureaucrat started addressing us. He spoke in a serious monotone and heavily accented English.

"Welcome to the USSR embassy in India. As you are well aware, the great country of India and the great country of Soviet Union are great friends. We are happy and proud to select talented students from across the world and provide them with great professional education. It is a great chance for all of you and I advise you to make the most of this great opportunity."

"If he says 'great' one more time, I will strangle him with my bare hands." Kevin hissed into my ears. I offered a nervous smile. I really did not want to miss a single word about this great opportunity. After all, it was my great chance!

I listened to Gromyko with rapt attention. I learned that all the selected students were going to be placed in different Russian medical colleges. We (the Bombay group) had been assigned to Leningrad University–the second largest university in Russia.

The programme terms were splendid. No fees throughout the 8-year course, free air tickets for our first entry and last departure and a student stipend of 90 Rubles per month, right from the first day!

As the 'great' introductory lecture came to an end, they handed us our air tickets to Moscow. We were scheduled to fly on 6th September!

Off to a new world of dreams and fantasies!

□□□

Up in the sky

September 6, 1985

Our taxi driver was trying his best to negotiate our cab through the weekend Delhi traffic to reach Palam airport. Our flight was scheduled to leave at 10.30 pm, so as per the rule book, we were trying to reach the airport at least three hours prior to departure. The slight drizzle and wind outside had made the taxi windows foggy. I felt claustrophobic.

My father was sitting beside me. Unlike his usual self, he was quiet, extremely quiet. He just sat there, tightly holding my hand and looking straight ahead. I too sat silently. It had been the same since the previous night, which we had spent at a distant relative's place. We had hardly spoken to each other during the farewell dinner. On the outside we were happy and cheerful, but it was a very different story inside.

I could well imagine his thoughts.

"My son is now going away to a foreign land with foreign customs. How is he going to cope there? Nobody is going to be there to guide him. Will he be able to manage on his own? Or will he stray?'

I did not have answers to any of these questions. I would have to find them on my own!

Hundreds of memories crowded my mind--our cosy flat, those family picnics, my childhood buddies, those small tiffs, those tiny triumphs, the sweaty smell of my father's shirt, the soft touch of my mother's sari, the mischievous twinkle in my sister's eyes. Distant, apparently forgotten memories, thoughts, sensations–all came rushing back only to remind me that I was leaving all this far behind, at least for the next eight years, if not forever! I tried to swallow the lump in my throat and sneaked a glance at my father–his eyes looked bloodshot.

The parting at the airport gate was made easier by the last minute chaotic activities.

"Check your passport...ticket is in the inner compartment of your pouch...don't forget about those $100...use them only for emergency. Write to us regularly...send the college and hostel telephone numbers...I will try and contact you whenever I can."

By now we had been joined by my Bombay mates, who were also going through the same routine with their fathers. With the final goodbyes and embraces over, we entered the airport! Suddenly the parting gloom disappeared and it was replaced by a sense of anticipation.

All of us were travelling by air for the first time and were overawed by the occasion. Luggage check-in, collection of boarding passes, immigration--each step seemed long and complicated, but soon everything got over without a hitch and we headed for the First Class Lounge. This luxury was thanks to Parag Shah's uncle, who was a senior officer at the airport.

Once inside the plush lounge, we whiled away our time watching television. Awkwardly we approached the attendants at the food and beverage counters, unsure whether we needed to pay or not. Suddenly Parag's uncle appeared. Smiling knowingly, he winked at us and said, "Don't worry about paying, it is free! *Abhee khaao piyo aish karo. Baad mein flight mein sirf khaakra khaana hai.*"

Though we were only too eager to oblige him, we did not get the khaakra reference! Didn't they serve food in international flights?

Just as our feasting on samosas, pastries and sandwiches was reaching its end, we heard the announcement.

"Passengers travelling on Aeroflot flight SU233 to Moscow are kindly requested to proceed to Gate No. 8 for boarding."

A chic Russian air hostess welcomed us aboard. There were almost 200 passengers aboard--barring a few Russian businessmen, the flight was full of young students, who were going to study in the USSR.

I was happy to get a window seat. Excited, I peered out of the window to see how the world outside looked. After watching the shadowy apron area, the waiting aircrafts, and the airport structures for about 15 minutes, my thrill waned. I was impatient to take off.

At last, the air hostess made an announcement for take-off. There was that noise of the whirring engines and the shuddering sensation of the purring plane, ready to glide into the air. I held on tightly to the armrest--not out of nervousness but in anticipation. I was ready to fly!

"Up here, up in the sky, come with me, I want to fly.
Don't stop, let the whole world know.
Don't stop, let the whole world know.
Come fast, come fast, don't be slow."

It is funny how some songs suddenly pop up, uninvited, in your mind and then just refuse to go away--even songs that you may have once ridiculed! The rather silly words of that *Ek Duje Ke Liye* number were now buzzing in my head. I could almost feel SP Balasubramaniam's heavy South Indian voice singing those words in my ears and despite serious attempts I just could not shake it off!

A few minutes later, we were in the sky and I was still humming the same silly lines.

"Up here, up in the sky, come with me, I want to fly.
Don't stop, let the whole world know.
Don't stop, let the whole world know.
Come fast, come fast, don't be slow."

□□□

Moscow, here I come!

All five of us were sitting in the same row. Though the hearty feast in the First Class Lounge had kept us quiet for quite a while, we soon grew hungry. So, when the food trolley arrived, our faces lit up. But it also brought with it the strong smell of meat, almost making us nauseous.

"Sir, Veg or Non-Veg?" The air hostess politely asked.

An orthodox *Gujju*, Parag Shah, shook his head violently and said, "No, thanks!"

He was already reaching for his backpack to take out his packet of *khaakras*! Suddenly, Parag's uncle's insinuation became crystal clear! Wise old man!

Kevin D'Souza, on the other hand, had decided to take the bull by the horn. "Boss, what are you thinking? When in *Roos*, eat like a Russian!" and then turning towards the air hostess, he said, "Give me non-veg please!"

The rest of us decided to follow his lead. . Yes, we did somehow survive that ordeal but as we struggled to push that strange, smelly food through our food-pipes, we all had some priceless expressions on our faces!

✣

"Come, let us go down." Yatin Patil nudged me. I looked at the others for consent. They nodded eagerly. Braving the chilly winds, we got down from the plane!

No, it was not Moscow, it was Tashkent. The plane had stopped at Tashkent airport for a two-hour refuelling break and it had been announced that passengers were allowed to move around within the airport premises.

For the next one and a half hours, we roamed around just like children in a toy shop. Excited at every new thing! The duty-free shops seemed to be full of inviting and expensive stuff. Our limited knowledge of Russian helped us in reading the signboards and trademarks. It felt good. Of course, there was no question of buying anything before reaching Moscow and we zealously guarded our wallets.

That was of course till Yatin Patil decided that it was show time! He dramatically picked up a carton of Dunhill cigarettes from a shelf and coolly paid its price in dollars. Looking triumphant, he declared, "Boss, now, bye bye Mumbai and *ta ta* India! No more restrictions, no more controls. I am going to start smoking from today."

The rest of us looked at him incredulously, drawing in a collective gasp!

✣

After going back to the plane, we sat in the empty back row. The reason was simple. Yatin wanted to smoke. The moment he expertly lit the cigarette and took his first puff, we knew that he was a pro in that art and no first-timer!

Yatin also specialised in dirty jokes, often plunging to the most dastardly depths of insanity and vulgarity! Just as we were laughing our guts off at one of his obnoxious tales, we were startled by the sound of feminine laughter. Looking up, we saw a young Indian air hostess, smiling down at us.

"So, all of you are from Bombay, huh? Going to study in Russia?" she asked.

My God! Was she listening to all our conversation?

All of us turned red with embarrassment. Thankfully, she decided to leave us but not before flashing a wicked grin. Looking sheepishly at each other, we laughed once again at the last joke's obnoxiously obscene punch-line!

The chatter went on for quite some time but then one by one we dozed off.

The PA system buzzed.

"In a short while from now, we will be landing at the Moscow's Sheremetyevo airport. The time there is 9 am and the local temperature is 12 degree Celsius. On behalf of Aeroflot, Commander Ivanchuk and his crew want to thank you and extend a warm welcome and wish you a happy stay in Moscow. Hope you have enjoyed your flight. Aeroflot is happy to serve you, always and forever!"

There was that all-too-familiar hollow feeling in the pit of my stomach. My heart seemed to be beating wildly. I had waited so long for this moment; I had worked so hard for this moment; and now finally that moment was here! I did not bother to peep out of the window. I wanted to feel Moscow.

"Moscow, here I come!"

□□□

The first impressions

September 7, 1985
Moscow 9.15 am

Huge, bright, and shiny... the Moscow airport dazzled us! Every inch of an impressive and imposing structure fit for the capital of a super-power nation. In spite of so many people moving around, it seemed to be extremely quiet, so much so that even our whispers sounded way too loud! Everything around us was moving just like clockwork. There were soldiers standing at every corner. With their crisp uniforms, ramrod stiff posture, and mask-like faces, they almost looked like decorative mannequins. The whole atmosphere felt thick with mystery and secrecy.

As I reached the immigration counter, the uniformed officer looked at me, unsmiling. He checked my passport details again and again. Then, in a gravelly voice, he told me to turn 180 degrees. Apparently, I was being photographed. He did not bother to say anything. Standing before him, I almost felt like an intruder, who would be whisked away any moment.

Iron curtain, persecution, prison, Siberia....

All conceivable negative thoughts started clouding my mind. After what seemed like an eternity, the officer gave me yet another penetrative gaze and finally stamped the entry-stamp on my passport. The loud thud made my heart skip a beat. There was not even a cursory 'Welcome'. With his steel grey eyes, he indicated the exit.

As I walked out, I realised I was actually trembling! Suddenly, I felt a strong urge to relieve myself. Summoning my limited

Russian reading skills, I finally managed to reach the washroom. The clean and bright restroom and the fresh smell of disinfectant somehow restored my faith in the efficiency of the Russian system. I relieved myself–both of the bodily wastes and my negative thoughts!

As expected, there was no water faucet in the toilet cubicle. I had already reconciled myself to losing that Indian 'luxury'! I told myself, "When in *Roos*, clean your ass like a Russian!" But lo behold! Where on earth was the toilet paper? There was no roll of toilet paper to be seen anywhere--only some printed squares of paper, stacked behind the commode. Just when I was about to put those papers to good use, I managed to make sense of the letters visible on one of the pieces.

Pravda.

Was it for real? Was I now going to use the Soviet Union's official newspaper as toilet paper? What did it mean? Was there a shortage of normal toilet paper in world's second Super-power's washrooms? Or was it just a part of some grand Socialist scheme of maximising utilisation of every possible community resource?

I stepped out of the cubicle, feeling a little dazed. Just then, Parag Shah came out from another cubicle. He was looking equally shocked.

He said, "*Arre yaar,* did you see that? The toilet paper?"

I nodded. Something made both of us look around to make sure that no one had seen or heard us. Luckily no one had—at least no one whom we could see!

✣

Around 80 of us had arrived in Moscow that day. We had been told that a group of senior students was going to pick us up from the airport. Two long hours later, three Indian-looking youngsters headed our way. Had our long wait finally come to a happy end? They came and enquired, "New batch?"

We eagerly replied, "Yes."

The tall, fair and handsome guy, standing in the middle, looked at us scornfully. With a smirk, he said, "Bloody Indians! Bloody bastard Indians!"

We were flabbergasted! With a satisfied snigger the trio walked off!

Thankfully, within the next 15 minutes our seniors arrived. A few of them were from Pune and we immediately bonded. When I narrated the incident of the trio calling us 'Bloody bastard Indians', one of them said, "Oh, that must be Ashish Aima. The bugger hates Indians!"

Ashish Aima- the name certainly sounded Indian. I just did not get it. But then very little had made sense since our arrival! Sighing, I quickly got into the bus.

✣

It was very cold outside. The windows were tightly shut to prevent the chilly wind from blowing in. Excited, I looked through the window, trying to engrave in mind my first visual impression of Moscow. It was autumn and even though it was around noon, it was dull and gloomy. The four-lane freeway, disciplined traffic, well-manicured landscapes, spotless cleanliness...everything seemed straight out of a Hollywood movie.

As soon as the bus entered the city, we saw a huge building complex. Parag exclaimed, "I think that must be Moscow State University. Remember, Anton studies there?"

Everyone laughed. The reference to Anton was an inside one. While taking our Russian courses, we had had a lesson about a boy named Anton, who studied in Moscow State University. The building we were now seeing was a perfect replica of the photograph in our textbook. All of us eagerly looked at 'Anton's Moscow State University', admiration writ large on every face! After a few minutes, Parag exclaimed, "Boss, look. Doesn't this building also look exactly like Anton's university building?"

All of us animatedly debated over which one was Moscow State University—the last one or the current one. But the game was yet to be over. The architects and town planners seemed to have done away with the concept of diversity; conformity seemed to be the order of the day. So, every five minutes we kept witnessing a similar, dull grey, huge building complex. By the time the *fifth*

Moscow State University appeared, we had given up hope of identifying the right one!

✣

Soon we reached our destination–a huge hotel in the university campus. There were about 200 students, who had come from different corners of the world, in the lobby. Black, white, yellow, brown–there was practically every race and every kind of face in that crowd. It looked as if we were standing in the midst of a miniature sea of humanity.

The hotel was going to be our residence till our respective universities sent the final confirmation. We were segregated into rows and told to collect our room keys from the front desk. While collecting the room keys we realised that our Bombay group had been split up. I had been assigned Room 1602 on the 16th floor while Parag had got 1401 on the 14th floor. Yatin, Kevin and Nilesh had been lucky to have been stacked together in 1203.

Tough, tall, soldierly-looking people were standing at every corner of the lobby. They were in plain clothes but it was quite clear that they were there to man us, to listen to every conversation, and to observe everyone. Having collected our room keys, we waited for our luggage to be transferred to our respective rooms. The excited chatter of the students gradually dwindled. Everyone had felt it–the big brother was watching us and watching us very closely!

"Give me your passports."

The loud announcement broke the uneasy silence in the lobby. It had come from one of our tough, tall 'observers'.

Hand over our passports? All of us looked at each other, bewildered.

"Foreign students, give me your passports please."

The announcement came again. He almost barked this time. In fact there was even more authority in his voice. The 'please' at the end was delivered as powerfully as a heavyweight boxer's punch. Reluctantly, we started fishing out our passports–the ultimate identification issued by our nation--from our backpacks and pouches and handed over our only proof of identity in a foreign land!

While giving my passport, I gathered the courage to ask, "Sir, when will we get our passports back?"

Without even bothering to look at me, he informed, "When you go to your college hostel."

Parag stuttered, "But Sir, till that time, what do we show as proof of identity?"

Now the plain clothed soldier looked irritated. Scowling, in his broken English, he replied, "No need passport. No show nothing. In the Soviet Union, no need identity. We know you, we know everything!"

Our very first lesson on the very first day--in the USSR there was no need of identity! How metaphorical! No individual identity in this society--only a collective one. Everyone was equal, everyone was same. Welcome to the faceless, race-less world of conformity! Hail Marx, hail Communism!

□□□

Another lesson

September 7, 1985
12.30 pm

The hotel lift was superfast. In less than a minute, I reached the 16th floor. The long corridor was empty besides my luggage that was kept neatly in front of my room--Room 1602.

Yes, that was the room assigned to me. I tried to open the door with my key but it was shut from inside. I could hear the sound of laughter coming from inside. After a minute's hesitation, I decided to knock.

"Yeah, *maan*? Who're you?'

The question had come from a giant of a black African guy, who was looking down at me quizzically. My throat seemed to dry up. Besides Hollywood movies, I had never seen such a tall and heavy black guy so close. That too, a near seven footer! Standing before him and feeling like a Lilliputian schoolboy, I introduced myself, "I am...I am Sadanand Borkar from India."

He smiled courteously. "India, huh? Come on *maan*. Come inside."

As I entered, I saw another African giant–even heavier and taller. He lay sprawling on the sofa. He also gave a friendly smile and pointed to an empty bed. So that was to be my sanctuary for two days and they were going to be my roommates!

Sitting down on the bed, I tried to comprehend their African accent and broken English but I was too alarmed to concentrate on what they were saying. I did not even get their names. The only thing I gathered from their rapid chatter is that they were from Barbados, West Indies. Though I kept smiling and nodding intermittently at what they were saying, my entire body was taut with fear. I kept imagining that at any moment, one of them would just leap at me and break my neck!

Fight being out of the question, flight was my only option... and without further ado I decided to take it. Biding my time, as they paused for two seconds, I excused myself and left the room. Closing the door behind me, I almost ran to the lift. Just as I was stepping inside the lift, I chanced to look behind--I saw one of them standing outside the room and frantically waving at me. Thankfully the lift door closed and I heaved a sigh of relief! I was praying hard.

'Save me God. Save me from this situation!'

✣

I got down at the 12th floor and headed to 1203. I had never felt happier to see the familiar faces of Yatin, Kevin and Nilesh. I began to calm down.

"What happened, *yaar*? You look so pale...and you are panting!" Yatin asked, closing the door. Before I could answer, someone started banging on their door. As Yatin opened the door, Parag rushed in. His face was white as a sheet. He was trembling like a leaf.

"What the f**k? What's happening, man? Can somebody please tell me what is going on here?"

A visibly shaken Kevin had hardly spoken these words when there was another loud knock on the door. It seemed as if suddenly everybody in the hotel had decided to come and knock on that door!

Puzzled, Yatin opened the door. I was startled to see my two West Indian roommates standing there, towering over us in their full glory. My heart skipped a beat! Why had they followed me? What did they want? I quickly glanced at my Bombay-buddies. They too looked petrified.

Finally, Kevin brought in a semblance of sanity. Offering a

handshake to one of the visitors, he asked, “Yes, boss. What’s up?” The ice was broken and our visitors smiled at us.

“Hey, *maan*, we just came to meet our roommate. Sadanand, right? We are leaving for Minsk right now, so just came by to say goodbye. Sorry, we couldn’t get to know each other better! Best of luck, Sadanand!”

All of us shook hands and bid goodbyes.

There was an uncomfortable silence in the room after they left. As we started chatting, I learned that Parag’s story was no different from mine. He had also fled from his room, just minutes after seeing his black African room-mates. He had also assumed them to be some homicidal maniac muggers out to get him!

Deep down, I was feeling horrible. How uptight and judgmental I had been in quickly labelling my new roommates as potential muggers, robbers and killers--and just because they were black and I was brown; they were tall and I was short; they were tough and I was not! Unlike me, the very same ‘muggers’ had shown courtesy and decency--they had come all the way just to bid me goodbye; they had even remembered my name from our tiny conversation! Till then I had always prided myself in being a polite and well-bred Indian...and here I was...a prejudiced soul! I burned with shame.

My stupidity and their friendliness had done me one good turn though--it had taught me to never judge a book by its cover!

□□□

The first night

September 7, 1985
3.30 pm

With my roommates gone, the room looked big and empty. Hours of travel and tension were taking a toll on me and I suddenly felt exhausted. The bed looked very inviting and in no time I was fast asleep.

My sleep was far from peaceful. I kept having one crazy dream after another. So, when I woke up with a start after a few hours, I was imagining that my plane had come crashing down on the ground. A wave of relief washed over me when I realised that the loud thud and commotion of the 'plane crash' was just someone banging on the door. The day seemed to be an unending series of knocking and banging!

Groggily, I got up to open the door. The Pune group of senior students, who had come to receive us at the airport, was standing there. One of the girls shouted chirpily, "Get ready sleepyhead. We are going on a half-day city tour. Tour, guide, and ice-cream–everything is on the house!"

Then, she gave me a close look from head to toe and said, "Not bad. Not bad at all for a junior!"

✣

The rest of the Bombay group was already waiting in the lobby. The excursion started with a visit to an ice-cream parlour on the same street. It was fun to eat ice-creams in the biting cold. As we newcomers admiringly watched Anish, one of our seniors, generously pay for the ice-creams, he winked at us and explained, "Boss, don't think too much of this. When you start getting your monthly 90 rubles, you'd know that paying for a five kopek ice-cream isn't a big deal!"

The seniors were quite familiar with the city and for the next two hours they took us trundling along to many different spots in the suburbs. As the sun set, the alluring alleys began to look increasingly menacing and sinister. It was not too hard to imagine a KGB agent snooping around.

Sunil, another senior, then took over, "Okay guys, let's wind up the tour. Let's get back to the hotel. We have to be back by 10 pm. It is already 7:20 pm. If we walk back, we will get late. Let's take the metro."

On our way to the metro station, he told us about Moscow's famous underground railway network, which ran at three levels–30 feet, 60 feet, and 90 feet; the stations were built like palaces; and it was extremely cheap!

✣

We entered a subway to go to our station. Long escalators kept taking us deeper and deeper underground, where I could see many intersecting corridors leading to different stations. Besides us, there was practically nobody there. The only sound seemed to be that of the occasional moving train. It seemed silent and creepy--straight out of a sci-fi movie.

I had fallen slightly behind the rest as my foot was hurting. The new shoe had caused blisters. With the pain becoming unbearable, I stopped to loosen and re-tie my shoelaces. When I finished and looked up, I was swept by panic. I could not see anybody from our group; in fact I was standing all by myself in a confusing maze of stairs and corridors!

I ran a few paces, shouting my friends' names but there was no response. Only the sound of my own voice reverberated. Frantic, I started running from one corridor to another but all were empty. There was not a soul in sight. By now I was sweating profusely. My senses had numbed and I started swearing loudly-

-the choicest expletives! I could not recall the name of the station nor the exact address of the hotel. I did not know enough Russian to ask for guidance and there was not a soul in sight, whom I could ask for help. Moreover, I was not carrying any identification or any money with me. In fact, I was not even carrying my wallet!

I just could not fathom what had happened. How could all my friends disappear so suddenly? Why was there nobody at any of these stations? What the hell was I supposed to do now? Was it some nasty prank?

A tap on my shoulder snapped me out of my reverie. As I turned around, I found myself looking into an 'Indian-looking' face.

He asked me with concern, *"O bhai-saab, kahaan jaanaa hai?"*

I felt weak with relief. I wanted to give him a tight hug! At last here was someone who would understand what I wanted and would be able to guide me. I explained my situation to him and asked him to help me. He patiently explained to me the way back to my hotel; which train, which line, which station–every tiny detail. I listened to him carefully. At the end of it I sheepishly asked, "Can you lend me some money? I don't have any!"

For a moment he looked suspicious, as he weighed his options about whether I was bluffing or not. Then he reached into his pocket and pulled out a note.

"Take this. Ten rubles. Should be enough."

As he turned to go, I said, *"Thank you bhai-saab. Kahaan se ho?* India?"

He smiled and said, "No, Pakistan!"

Tears welled in my eyes. Once again, I learnt that prejudices were stupid. My natural lifelong aversion to anything Pakistani, my longstanding belief that they hated us and were our staunch enemies was replaced by gratitude and faith in the innate goodness of the human race.

Tightly holding that 10-ruble note, I started walking towards the corridor he had shown. Just when I was about to reach the ticket window, I heard animated voices from behind.

"Look, there he is...going towards the ticket window!"

My group had suddenly reappeared. A full 45-minute train

journey later they had realised that I was not with them!

Once again, I swore loudly at them, but this time I was smiling with sheer relief!

✣

"Baby, don't be upset. Such things do happen. Come on. Cheer up."

The girl, who had chirpily woken me up that afternoon, had now taken over the role of being my personal cheerleader. After dinner, one by one all my friends and seniors left but not her. She still lingered on. I enjoyed the extra attention.

"Come on, there is a coffee shop in the hotel. Let us have coffee," she invited.

After the coffee, I bid her goodnight but she insisted on seeing me off till my room. As we entered my room, a strange sensation started tickling my nerves.

Standing at the door, she asked, "Hey, where're your roommates?"

As I recounted what had happened earlier that day, she started laughing. I looked at her fascinated.

She was rather good looking and was looking lovelier by the minute as she laughed! Suddenly she stopped laughing, closed the door, and sat down right next to me on the bed. Feeling her warm body next to me, my heart started beating faster.

Before I could say anything, she started removing our clothes--first hers and then mine. My mind was swirling. Inside me, a hundred conflicting emotions were raging. I was shocked, I was thrilled. I was afraid, I was eager. I wanted to run away, I wanted to remain rooted.

Crooning sweet nothings into my ears, as she expertly started working me over, I could not help thinking about all the drama that had unfurled over the day. Within just 24 hours, Moscow had changed my life forever. I felt on top of the world!

Through the feelings of ecstasy, the girl kept cooing in my ear.

"Not bad. Not bad at all for a junior!"

□□□

Off to Rostov

September 8, 1985
10.30 pm

From midnight ecstasy to mid-morning agony is but a mere journey of few hours!

At that moment, I was precisely experiencing this irony of life. All of us were huddled together in the lobby, where a Russian official was announcing the travelling schedules of students. He had just announced that our Bombay-group had been split. In the early afternoon, Yatin, Nilesh, and Kevin were to leave for Leningrad State University, while I and Parag would leave for Rostov State University in the late afternoon.

The five of us had grown quite close in the previous two years. Together, we had gone through the rigours of learning Russian; together we had planned our Russian odyssey; and together we had arrived there. Now, instead of moving together to Leningrad, two of us had been unexpectedly told to go to Rostov. None of us had even heard of that university before!

As the Leningrad and Rostov groups parted ways, Parag and I cursed Russia and the Russians under our breath. A tall, bespectacled guy, wearing a fancy cap and standing next to us, suddenly interrupted our grumbling with, "Hi, I am Sanjay Gupta from Delhi. I am also going to Rostov."

I shook his hand and asked, "Have you any idea about Rostov? I have never heard of that place. We were supposed to go to Leningrad. This has come as a nasty surprise."

Sanjay laughed and said, "You are not going to Leningrad simply because some high-level politician must have pushed his candidate over you. Tough luck, mate. It seems your 'pull' was not enough."

Indignant, I said, "Boss, I did not use anybody's pull to come here. I am here on merit."

Immediately sensing my annoyance, he said, "Ok boss, I was just telling you what could have happened. Anyway, don't lose heart. There is plenty to look forward to in Rostov."

My curiosity piqued and I eagerly asked, "Really? What are you talking about?"

He grinned widely and said, "Rostov has a very strong Turkish influence. The girls there are among the most beautiful ones in Russia--a perfect mix of Russian and Turkish genes. My cousin, who is studying there, has informed me that they are easy to get!"

My nocturnal encounter was still fresh in my mind and the possibility of more such rendezvous made me smile! In an instant, my despondency about Rostov gave way to anticipation!

✣

At exactly 5 pm, we left for the railway station in a bus. Sitting in the train to Rostov, I immediately became aware of how different they were from the trains back home. This train looked like the plush Orient Express from a long forgotten movie. It had many bogies with interconnecting long corridors, private coupes, comfortable berths, and a separate dining salon. Going with the Class-less Communist philosophy, there were no separate first, second, or third class compartments. Yet the overall standard of the compartments was much superior to Indian Railways' first class.

Each compartment was looked after by a uniformed lady, who played the dual role of a conductor-cum-caretaker. Our conductor was a buxom beauty in her thirties, who checked our tickets with a deliberate flourish and departed after flashing a melting smile. Smile! Yes, here, for the first time, I saw Russians smiling at us amicably. In fact, the Russians travelling with us seemed very friendly. It was indeed a welcome relief after our cold encounters with grim, unsmiling Russian officials.

As the train moved on, I kept looking at the blurry landscape. Slowly the skyline of Moscow disappeared. The city that had changed my life in a day vanished away!

✣

We decided to have dinner at 9 pm. Within two days, I had got quite used to Russian sandwiches and butter-broths (pronounced *butyer broth*). Even the smell of raw meat now seemed perfectly acceptable. Parag, however, was still not over the food culture shock. So, he kept munching on his *khaakras* and *theplas*!

With his cap on, Sanjay Gupta was looking a lot like Dev Anand in Jewel Thief and then he did something that the evergreen superstar would typically have done in his movies. He took out a guitar from his luggage case and started singing a Kishore Kumar number. Hearing his fresh and youthful voice belting out *Jeevan ke safar mein raahee milte hain bicchad jaane ko* brought an indescribable surge of homesickness. But soon nostalgia gave way to a party mood. The strains of music seemed to have transformed the entire compartment. There were quite a few Russian youngsters in our compartment and they joined in enthusiastically. They seemed to be thoroughly enjoying Hindi songs and even tried to sing with us in broken Hindi. Then one of them surprised us with a tuneful rendition of the Russian version of the song *Aawara hoon*. He explained to us–half in English, half in Russian--that this Mukesh song and Raj Kapoor were perennial favourites of Russians.

The singing soiree had cheered us up considerably. Once again that top of the world feeling was coming back to me. As if to boost that delusion, a Russian beauty came near me and conspiratorially asked, "*Jimmy Jimmy*?" Her voice was hoarse. Her breath smelled of alcohol.

I was stumped. I had no clue what she wanted.

Then she wiggled her waist and asked, "Don't know *Jimmy Jimmy*?"

Baffled, I kept looking at her while wracking my brains in an effort to guess what she meant. My mind was racing. I was weighing different options. Was she really suggesting what I thought she was? But how could she? Didn't she know that we were in a crowded train compartment? What should I do now?

Exasperated, she asked, "Don't know Mithun? Mithun Chakraborty?"

Oh, so that was what she wanted. All my raunchy thoughts vanished in an instant. I realised that she just wanted me to sing that awful song from *Disco Dancer!* But hey, who cared about the aesthetics of that song? If she had asked for it, I would give it to her. I started singing *Jimmy Jimmy Jimmy Aajaa Aajaa*. The party once again came alive with everyone joining in!

As I finished, the girl said, "Lovely song!"

She pecked me on the cheek and made me a take a sip from her glass--my first sip of Russian Vodka or any liquor for that matter! The burning bitter taste made me feel as if my brain was going to explode. As I started coughing violently and tears welled in my eyes, the girl laughed naughtily. In her sexy, husky voice, she said, "Welcome to Soviet Union!"

It was a 'warm' welcome indeed!

✣

Next morning began with the typical muffled noises of people moving about the compartment--some getting ready to alight, some pulling their luggage trolleys, some asking the conductor-lady for assistance. Someone raised the curtain at the window and sunlight poured in. Rubbing my eyes, I reluctantly got up. The first view of the Russian countryside just took my breath away. I was looking at an unending expanse of golden yellow wheat. Never before had I seen such a huge field--it seemed to be running on and on for acres.

"We are now passing Ukraine, one of the biggest producers of wheat in the world. See those huge crop-cutting machines, they are called combines. Look at those churches with domes. Do you see those slightly twisted crosses along with the downturned half-moon crescents? Those peculiar crosses are there as symbols to signify the Russian Czar's victory over Islamic aggressors."

I looked at Sanjay with unabashed admiration. He seemed to have done his homework on Russia and Rostov. He had also done one more thing--with his outgoing and friendly nature and his love for music, he had found a friend in me for life!

Then and there I decided that, given a choice, I would opt to share the hostel room in Rostov with him!

□□□

The arrival

September 9, 1985
3.30 pm

Our 22-hour train journey was finally coming to an end. We were reaching Rostov station. We were the last batch to arrive. Before us, about 70 students had already reached Rostov. The official bus was waiting outside the station to take us to Rostov State University's medical college.

The bus dropped us at the college gate. Both the medical college and the hostel were situated in a huge complex of around a dozen buildings. Most of the buildings looked old and grey. Later we got to know that many had been there since the time of World War I. The main building, however, was a spanking new one and looked like an obvious later addition. We were told that it housed all the important offices. So, our dean, rector and the heads of the departments would all sit there. New country, new college, new teachers–I was savouring the thrill of a new beginning!

A tired looking old man guided us into the convention hall, where the rector and the dean were going to address us newcomers. Both men were tall, overweight, and red. Red was not only the colour of their skin but also their thoughts. Both of them kept peppering their boring welcome speeches with repeated mention of Vladimir Lenin. I don't think any of us completely understood their flowery speeches, but it was evident that they were highlighting the greatness of Soviet teaching traditions and the important role their university was playing in providing higher education to students across the world.

We clapped enthusiastically at the end of each speech, more out of relief than appreciation.

After the introductory speeches were over, we were taken to a small hall for hostel room allocation. The long train journey was gradually taking a toll on us and we were eager to get to our rooms. Sanjay and I were a little late to join the group, most of which had dutifully taken their seats in the hall. We decided to stretch our limbs and just stand near the door. We were chatting merrily in Hindi and guffawing loudly, making fun of the two boring college bosses when an authoritative voice came from behind, *"Namaste! Toh aap India se hain?"*

Startled by the perfect Hindi, we turned around to see a tall, formidable-looking, bespectacled Russian lady looking at us. She had the reddest hair we had ever seen. We looked at her meekly. Why did we have to talk all that crap about the rector and the dean? Just because we thought nobody would understand Hindi? Well, it was quite clear that we were terribly wrong to assume that.

As we stood with our dead duck expression, expecting her to tell us to pack up and leave, she broke into a broad smile. Extending a handshake, she said, "I am Juliana Shepilova, your hostel rector and class teacher. Nice to meet you!"

Both of us offered her limp handshakes and mumbled pleasantries. Sensing our discomfort, she decided to put us out of our misery and said, "Don't worry. It's okay. Go inside and join your class."

Without another word we went into the hall. By then, the back benches had been filled up and the only places left for us were on the first bench! So we sat there, waiting for the room allocation to begin.

'Gingerhead Juliana', as she was popularly known on the campus, had made an instant impression on us. She seemed to be a kind and understanding teacher, who knew exactly when to crack the whip and when to cut the slack! We had already promised ourselves that we would not be caught fooling around ever again.

Later, she pleasantly surprised us by allotting Indian students the new wing that had been built just a few months back. It had been freshly painted and had nice rooms, a perfect central heating system and brand new furniture. Many others from our batch, mostly the students from Africa and the Far East, got rooms in the old wings.

Sanjay and I were allocated Room Number 12. We were to share it with another Russian student, who was scheduled to join us later. It was a spacious room with a wall-to-wall carpet. There were three steel beds with good mattresses and thick, full-length blankets. With a strong steel cupboard, three tables, and three chairs, the room looked perfectly functional. A probe-like smoke detector was placed on the ceiling.

Sanjay quietly pointed to that and hissed, "Stay out of its range. Everyone says it is the KGB's secret camera!"

✣

Later that evening, we found out the secret of Gingerhead's fondness for Indian students and her mastery over Hindi. As a part of our orientation program she had invited all the new students for tea at her quarters. Her house--a small bungalow on the campus--looked like a museum, a Nehru-Gandhi museum! All the walls were full of photographs of Mahatma Gandhi, Jawaharlal Nehru, and Indira Gandhi.

Juliana filled us in on her life. "I studied in Gorakhpur on a student exchange programme. I was teaching Russian there for three years. That is when I learnt to speak Hindi. I even met Indiraji in Delhi. Look at that photograph."

All of us looked at an enlarged, framed photograph showing a young and good-looking Juliana giving a bouquet of flowers to Indira Gandhi.

She proudly said, “Look, she has even signed this photograph. What a great lady! Such a good friend of Russia! How could someone just spray bullets on her?” She sounded choked with emotion.

I looked at Sanjay and gave a ‘now-we-know’ kind of look!

The tea party went off well. While bidding us goodnight, Gingerhead reminded us, “Remember, the lectures start at 8 am sharp. Be there on time!”

We dutifully nodded our heads. My medical career was finally set to begin!

□□□

Adjustment

The first year syllabus was extremely boring to say the least. We were just rehashing our twelfth standard physics, chemistry and biology; polishing our Russian language skills; and learning about Communism! It was just a preparatory course and had nothing interesting or nothing even remotely connected to Medicine.

On the other hand, hostel life was turning out to be quite exciting. It had the four things that I had always longed for--fun, frolic, friends and freedom! A midnight ragging session in the first week had proved to be the unexpected ice-breaker. With ten different seniors coming from ten different countries asking questions like 'Favourite heroine...favourite girl in the class... their approximate 'sizes'...favourite fantasies... shagging time... shagging methods....' it had been the usual guy ragging stuff. We had played along and everyone had had good fun. In the end, the same seniors had turned into our best friends. Now, they were taking us around the city's hot spots; giving us tips about avoiding the worst Mithun Chakraborty movies (the only Hindi movies that ever came to Rostov!) and telling us stale jokes about the city's famous Golden Girl statue!

Initially there was bit of a hiccup about the fifth thing that I longed for--'Food'! But with every passing week, even that problem vanished. I had begun to realise one thing--Russia was slowly not only changing me from the outside, but also from the inside. Craving for Indian food and Indian spices was gradually becoming a thing of past. My taste buds had grown quite comfortable with Russian soups, salads, sandwiches, and

'Smetana' (a thick, sour creamy dairy product). I was quite happily devouring the canteen's insipid lunches and dinners of mashed potatoes, boiled meats, and characterless gravies. Gulping down vodka and wine had also become a regular habit.

Another thing that helped us a great deal in our seamless integration into Russian life-style was our educational field trips!

✣

Some wise old Russian soul had decided that foreign students should be regularly taken out on educational field trips to interact with the local population in order to integrate them with the local culture and customs. It was a great idea!

Many of Russia's topmost writers and scientists had either lived or worked in Rostov or nearby towns. So, very often our trips were to visit the houses and workplaces of these legends. It was a wonderful experience visiting places frequented by the likes of Tolstoy, Gorky, Chekov, Pushkin, Sokholov, Mendeleyev and Pavlov. The sense of history there was simply overwhelming. We, however, preferred to visit places frequented by common Russian people--like government offices, factories, and colleges. Of these, our most favourite hangout was of course the Nursing College!

Yes, you heard it right–the Nursing College! My God, what hot chicks--all single and more than willing to mingle! We sometimes felt as if they were all officially primed to do so, but hey, who cared? If that was someone's idea of hooking up the global student community to Russian culture, then it was hard to find fault with his logic. History had enough examples to show that the lure of curvaceous beauties had more often than not proved too hard to resist!

No wonder then that these weekly field trips went on to become the high points of our life in Rostov and considerably added to our understanding of Russian culture and customs!

✣

Accepting Russian girls was one thing and accepting Igor

Tarasov, our Russian roommate, was quite another! Every room had at least one Russian student and we had got Igor. Officially speaking, these Russian partners were there for the same lofty reason--to ensure our integration with the Russian language and Russian people--but almost every expatriate student had this healthy suspicion that it was KGB's dirty idea to keep a tab on us. Indian students had even given these Russian students a code name—*'Natthu'*. The system came in quite handy. While talking about something sensitive, if a Russian student was spotted approaching, then somebody would just said, *"Chup ho jaao boss. Natthu aa rahaa hai."* (Shut up. *Natthu* is coming!) and everyone would go silent.

But Igor was not like any other *Natthu*. He won us over with his frankness and command over English. He was a fun guy, who kept regaling us with Russian jokes and real life anecdotes. He was usually busy chasing girls and hardly showed any interest in what we were doing. So it was hard to see him as a KGB-planted mole! The only time he bothered us was when he brought one of his many girlfriends to our room. Then he would mischievously wink at us and we would make ourselves scarce!

Bringing girls to the room (and wining, dining, and bedding them!) was not barred in our hostel. The unwritten rule was simple. 'What you do in your free time is your own prerogative. Just make sure you don't bring the roof down!' In due course of time, we too learned to enjoy the fruits of this 'Live and let live' policy! To cut a long story short, we adjusted to the new environment rather well!

□□□

Long live Soviet Union!

As time passed we got to know more and more people both on and off the campus. So, the weekends started to become more interesting. On most Saturday nights we were either busy shaking a leg in the makeshift discotheques sprouting up on every floor of the hostel or visiting some Indian friends staying in other places for late-night dinners.

The nightout picnics were even better. These only happened when either Igor or some other Russian friend managed to borrow his father's or brother's car for the weekend. Then we would set out with foldable tents, fishing lines, and packed food to camp in the riverside woods. The cool breeze, the starry nights, and the forest sounds made for an exotic, eerie cocktail of serenity and wilderness, making us feel as if we were in a totally different world. Forest, fresh air, fishing, booze, and barbecue! What more could we want?

One such nightout picnic brought for me the first official warning from Gingerhead Juliana!

✣

That nightout had been a particularly wild one. We had organised a rowing competition to go with the 'who-drinks-the-most-vodka' contest. The aftereffect of that exertion and exhaustion (not to mention the splitting hangover!) had been so great that on reaching the hostel, I had slept like a log.

A nightmare was on...I was wandering like a zombie in the jungle... surrounded by dark shadows...consumed by fear...running away from something sinister. But however hard I tried to run, that thing still kept chasing me. All of a sudden there were heavy footfalls behind me. They kept getting louder and louder.

I woke up with a start.

Thankfully, it proved to be the standard Russian soundscape–loud thuds on my room door!

I opened the door in a daze but one look at the person standing outside immediately brought me to my senses. Gingerhead Juliana was standing outside, looking much like a raging bull with flared nostrils. Looking behind her and seeing the number of half-naked, dishevelled students standing in the corridor, I safely assumed that she had already banged on at least 10 to 12 doors on our floor. I shuffled over to join the group and waited for her tirade to begin.

Julianna's outburst seemed like a machine-gun's staccato fire. "Do none of you have any sense of timing? It is 9 am. In another half an hour the Revolution Day parade will begin. I had already told you the day before yesterday that today all of you are supposed to be at Theatre Square by 8:30am. How could you just ignore my instructions? It is gross indiscipline. This won't be tolerated. The next time I find you doing this, you will find yourself on the next plane out of Russia. Now get ready and join the parade in 15 minutes. You heard it, 15 minutes and not a minute more!"

✣

Getting ready in a jiffy, all of us rushed to Theatre Square. The huge square was teeming with people. Everyone was wearing bright outfits, carrying colourful placards, and shouting patriotic slogans. The whole atmosphere was electric--one could almost feel the intense patriotic fervour everywhere. Then the parade began to the rhythmic sounds of drums and other instruments. World War II veterans led the parade, followed by young students, soldiers, policemen, firemen, and cultural troupes. The youngsters danced deliriously, alongside. It was almost like a merry carnival. Frenzied chants and hand-held posters celebrated their beliefs.

'Long live Lenin!'

'Long live Revolution!'

'Long live Communism!'

'Long live Soviet Union!'

It was not long before all of us joined in the mass hysteria, as we shouted ourselves hoarse with 'Long live Lenin'...'Long live Revolution'.... 'Long live Communism'... 'Long live Soviet Union!'

I sneaked a glance at Gingerhead Juliana. She was watching us from afar; beaming with pride.

All was well with Soviet Union!

□□□

Winter shopping

"Hey, sleepyhead, get up. We have to go to *Univer-Mag* today. Did you forget or what? It is our winter-shopping day."

I was barely 20 minutes into my afternoon siesta when Sanjay woke me up by literally yanking away my blanket. Yes, I had almost forgotten that entry on our calendar. It was already November and winter had set in. It was time for us to prepare ourselves for the bone-chilling Russian cold. We had already learnt that the sweaters and warm clothes that all of us had got from home would be totally useless in warding off the Russian winter. The Russian winter had always been unsparing and all those who had been foolish enough to take it lightly had greatly suffered. The bitter lessons learnt by ambitious aggressors like Napoleon and Hitler now served as warning signals for novices like us. Gearing up for temperatures up to minus twenty centigrade was indeed serious business and so we were being officially taken for our winter-shopping!

✣

On the way to *Univer-Mag*, I remembered the first warning that I had received about the severity of Russian winter from a senior on my first day at Rostov. We had just finished admiring our room, when a senior came in to give us some paper rolls and said, "*Insulyatsia.*"

The blank look on our faces prompted him to explain. "Insulate the windows properly by sticking these paper strips. Seal all the gaps so that cold air does not enter the room. Even though these rooms are centrally heated and the windows have double-layered glasses, the slightest exposure to those extreme cold winds can freeze you to death."

We had promptly set about sticking the paper strips to seal the gaps in the windows. The insulation process, however, was no easy task since glue was out of stock and we had to use a sticky soap bar as a substitute! But still everyone did as asked. No one wanted to be found frozen to death the next morning!

✣

'Universalniy Magazin' or *Univer-Mag* was the Russian supermarket. Although it was a huge building with many sections that stacked all sorts of items, one thing was quite striking. Everything looked remarkably drab and dull. There was no elegance or sparkle that one routinely associated with things 'foreign'. Even the small grocery back home boasted of better-packaged goods.

With dull grey walls and dim lighting, the whole atmosphere felt strangely gloomy. There were no advertisement posters or leaflets. There was no buxom beauty flashing her white teeth to promote a toothpaste, or a muscular hero showing off his well-groomed hair to sell a hair cream.

I asked Igor, "Don't you have any advertisements?"

He just rolled his eyes in disgust. "Advertisements? What for? It is all capitalist nonsense! If people want to buy something, they will go and buy that thing. Why unnecessarily promote those things? Such needless acts go on to corrupt people's minds."

I nodded my head meekly–more in shock, than in agreement. There was a sly smile on Sanjay's face!

Igor's sentiments were apparently shared by all Russian salesmen at *UniverMag*. They believed that if people wanted to buy something, then they would simply go ahead and buy that thing, so, no one took any effort to guide or convince us to shop!

✣

The winter apparel section was well-stocked. Igor was our

advisor and he advised us to first pickup our winter shoes. More than ankle-length in height and lined with a thick layer of wool inside, each leather shoe weighed more than a kilogram. After wearing them, for a moment I felt as if I was completely stuck to the ground...walking easily in them was definitely going to take quite a while.

Then we picked up full-length overcoats and some pairs of gloves and socks. Thick cotton or leather on the outside and wool on the inside seemed to be the norm for all winter apparels. Then we went to check out the most interesting item on our shopping list–the *shapka* (a big fur hat with earflaps).

Igor guided us, "Choose your *shapka* carefully. You cannot tackle Russian winters without it. Go for a rabbit fur one, it is the best. You can either tie the flaps at the top or at the chin. In extreme cold, you can cover your whole face with a chin-flapped *shapka* and just leave a small slit to see through. When every breath you exhale forms tiny sharp icicles, no protection is quite enough!"

✣

Armed to take on the harsh Russian winter, we soon got used to wearing all those accessories and did not feel their weight. After using them, we were unanimous in our verdict, "Whoever had first designed those things were brilliant!"

Despite the plummeting temperatures outside, our winter accessories made us feel as if we were walking around with our personal heating system!

□□□

A night to remember

November 19, 1985

"Hey, who is making all that noise?" Annoyed, I asked Sanjay.

He just shrugged to convey that he had no clue. Dinner was over and we were ready to retire for the night. But the loud noise outside was posing a hindrance. And it was only becoming louder and louder. It was coming from the direction of the city square, which was just outside our hostel premises. There were loud jubilant shouts and whoops like the ones you hear after a big football or cricket match victory. Our curiosity piqued and we both swooped down to the city square with our friends.

It was freezing cold outside. The square was dark, except for the faint moonlight. But from that deep, dark night-sky millions of tiny, fluffy, white snowflakes were coming down. Besides their ice-cold touch, there was little to distinguish them from wisps of soft white cotton. Swaying crazily like drunken ballerinas, those snowflakes swiftly enveloped the entire landscape in a thick layer of snow! For a person, whose knowledge of snow flakes originated from movies and books, it seemed like a fairytale!

As I stood mesmerised, a rather large snowball struck me squarely on the forehead and brought me to my senses. Just as I was about to attribute it to Mother Nature's design, a bigger snowball crashed onto my chest and within seconds another hit me in the face. By now I was certain that someone was using me as a soft, unsuspecting target. My only solace was that even my friends were getting bombarded. Soon we tracked down the attackers. The nursing college girls, who were out on the street enjoying the season's first snowfall, seemed to have taken a special fancy towards us! Spotting the girls, we countered them with equal enthusiasm and fervour.

Meanwhile, an enterprising guy from our hostel brought down a huge washing tub and placed it at the centre of the street. It was then filled up with vodka, gin, beer, wine, apple juice, and whatever beverage one could find in the hostel. There weren't enough glasses but no one cared. Everyone drank the stuff with cupped hands. It was a cocktail party like never before; for it was a night like never before!

The nursing girls were anyway partial towards medical guys and within no time, we were singing and dancing; and building all sorts of snow-figurines together. It was fun—absolute and unadulterated fun!

Out of the blue, a tall Russian girl grabbed me by the collar. She was totally drunk and I too was on the very last stage of sobriety. When she said, "Hey you, come here. Hold me tight," I never had to do anything at all--she held me tight, almost choking me to death, and kissed me through the slits of the chin-covering *shapkas*. And then, our first snowfall celebration went on and on, late into the moonlit night, right on that snow-covered street of Rostov!

✣

The next day began with a terrible hangover and the bitter realisation that it was past 10 am. I or for that matter, the entire Indian juniors group had already missed the first two periods. Fearing the worst from Gingerhead Juliana, we nervously trudged to class. On reaching, however, we received a pleasant surprise. Juliana was there alright but she was not looking particularly angry. In fact, she greeted us with a sarcastic, knowing smile.

"Oh, here come our adventurous Indians. So boys, how have you been? Enjoyed the snowfall last night? Met up with some nice nursing students? Had snow fights? Made a cocktail in a wash-tub?"

Each of her questions was loaded with a definite 'I-know-exactly-what-you-had-been-up-to' look. Even though she was smiling sweetly, her smile conveyed one thing clearly. The big brother was watching and reporting our each and every move. One more wrong move and we would be thrown out for sure. We kept quiet. With a false laugh to conceal her irritation, Juliana called us in and proceeded with the lecture as if nothing had happened!

□□□

The winter escapades

"Bloody Russian winter!" hissed Sanjay, as he settled on his bed.

"What has happened now?" I asked. He was just back after meeting his senior friend, who was working in the emergency section.

Sanjay was just waiting to explode and he did. "Have you ever visited the emergency section of our hospital? It is simply impossible to work there nowadays. The roads have turned into slippery sheets of ice. Old people are breaking bones by slipping while walking and the youngsters are skidding their cars and hitting lampposts while driving. It is absolute mayhem! The casualty doctors are going crazy. They literally have no other work except to tend to these winter accidents!"

I nodded in agreement. There was no soft, flaky snow on the roads; just smooth, transparent and slippery sheets of ice. Walking and driving on those ice sheets was a nightmare. The municipal workers would often come and sprinkle industrial salt to melt the ice into softer snow so that it could be shovelled away, but those measures were hardly enough. Many times the city's traffic would come to a complete halt for hours after a heavy snowfall.

As if on cue, Fadi, our Lebanese friend, knocked and informed, "Hey guys, the road traffic has come to a standstill outside our hostel. Since it is Sunday, our profs have decided that all boarders should help clear the snow from the clogged roads."

Community work was an important part of our syllabus and we enthusiastically responded to that call of duty. It was action time!

We began working in high spirits. Standing shoulder-to-shoulder with the professors, we started shovelling the snow away.

By 3.30 pm the heavy cloud cover had made it very dark. We had already managed to clear quite a few kilometres of the road and had reached a nearby woody area. We sang songs, sipped vodka, and egged each other on. It was almost a festive atmosphere!

All of a sudden, a strong beam of light, that almost blinded us with its intensity, descended from the sky and encircled our group. A near-deafening, whirring sound told us that a helicopter, possibly an army one, was hovering menacingly above our heads!

"Stop work immediately. Do not move from your place. I repeat. Stop work immediately. Do not move from your place."

The loud megaphone announcement stopped us dead in our tracks. Within minutes, we found ourselves surrounded by three military trucks. Commandoes carrying machineguns hurriedly descended from the trucks and stood around us in guarding position.

We stood there, stunned. No one knew what was happening. Were we being arrested? Had we trespassed into some forbidden land? We kept looking at each other, searching for answers. But even our professors looked totally clueless.

"Form a straight line and get into the trucks. Now." A commando barked.

We walked in a hurriedly formed queue and got into the trucks. No one said a word. The trucks brought us to our hostel campus. A few minutes later we heard two thunderous explosions. They had come from the woody area we had just left!

"What is happening?" One of our professors finally summoned the courage to ask the leader of the commandoes.

He explained, "Landmines...from World War II...many of them are still live. The woods were to be cleared of these live landmines today but you guys went there before us. You are lucky the helicopter spotted you! That must have been the bomb squad blowing up the live mines!"

So, that was the emergency. Even in the sub-zero temperature, I found myself sweating profusely. Fate had intervened at the nick of time. Otherwise it could well have been one unexpected boom and everything going silent forever!

✣

The winter became harsher. The days became extremely short. The sun would be barely seen for a few hours, as night would set in at 4 pm. The sky remained grey and gloomy and the earth became a vast sheet of white. No other colour was visible for miles. Going outdoor became almost impossible. Except for the weekend grocery visits, everyone preferred to remain indoors. All these changes took a heavy toll on many people, including many of my classmates. Depression became rampant on the campus. Sad, long faces, monosyllabic sentences, and teary nostalgic reminiscences of homelands became the order of the day or rather the order of the season.

Thankfully, I coped well with this extreme weather. It was all thanks to my roommates. Both Sanjay and Igor were always cheerful and they could lighten any mood with their sense of humour. They taught me the essential art of washing blues away with laughter!

✣

To keep us cheerful, the college often organised various field trips. But when simple acts like breathing and speaking produce a spray of sharp icicles, field trips can hardly bring any cheer. Yet there was one trip that I will never forget.

We were taken to a beach near the Sea of Azov. Teary-eyed Tatiana was our in-charge that day. Temperatures had dropped down drastically. The beach sand was almost blanketed by snow. The blue sea could not be seen. Tatiana suddenly left the group and started walking gingerly on a freshly formed sheet of ice. After walking for about a hundred metres, she stopped and marked the spot with a stick. Turning towards us, she shouted, "All of you carefully walk till the spot marked by the stick. Remember one thing, you are going to be walking on the Sea of Azov. The seawater has frozen. Don't venture ahead like fools. It is not safe. The snow there is thin. It might give in and we have no divers to fish out bodies from the bottom of the sea!"

Walking on the sea? We looked at each other incredulously. Surely this was going to be another first in life. Sanjay walked ahead of us. He was the first one to reach the spot marked by the stick and then suddenly, he just disappeared!

For a moment all of us were terror-stricken and were about to scream for help, when we heard his cheerful voice from behind a heap of snow.

"Come on guys, come here. Look what I've found out. If you pee here, the urine stream freezes into ice. Come on, give it a try."

The next moment, we were standing in a row, some 30 of us, peeing together, adding our two cents to the vast expanse of frozen salty water of the Sea of Azov. Sanjay was right—our urine was indeed turning into ice within seconds! In the famed history of Russian winters, all of us had contributed our legendary piece; I mean pees!

□□□

Hail Communism!

The old man standing on the dais droned on and on about Marx, Engels, Lenin, the history of Soviet Union, the Communist Party and how Communism was the best social system in the world. In his long black coat, flowing white beard, and whiskered white moustache, he looked a mirror image of Tolstoy or some similar gentleman from that era. He mumbled as if he was talking to himself. Serene and calm, devoid of any passion or fire, he looked like an old sage at complete peace with the world! For some time I tried hard to concentrate on what he was trying to teach us. But his dull, dreary talk slowly started drowning my senses and sitting on the last bench, I peacefully dozed off.

Molotov's lectures on Communism were like that!

✥

How could this man have a name like Molotov? Isn't that the name of the scientist who invented an explosive mix called the 'Molotov cocktail'? How can you even say the words 'Molotov' and 'explosive' in the same breath? Almost every student in our college had come up with a wisecrack or two about that paradox. They had even been uncharitable enough to say such things within his earshot. But Molotov had taken all that in his leisurely stride and had never lost his composure. Ultimately all of us had arrived at the same conclusion.

"Forget it, it doesn't matter. He is a good man!"

✥

The reasons for calling Molotov a good man were many. One, he never took attendance; two, he never bothered about whether anybody was listening to him or not; three, he never disturbed a sleeping student; and four, he never failed anyone! Despite his 'All Pass' record (or rather because of that), students never bothered studying Communism, Socialism and all the other related stuff. His classes were just meant for mass bunking, gossiping, or napping.

When it came to Communism exams, the advice from Indian seniors to juniors was simple, *"Parchi banana, yaar!"* Everyone just did that and made merry!

For the uninitiated, I must explain. *'Parchi banana'* was not some form of banana. In colloquial Hindi it referred to the rather elaborate process of making tiny paper-chits; writing bullet point answers of expected exam-questions on them; hiding them imaginatively (in places like shirt-collar, shirt-sleeves, secret pockets, belt buckles, elastic strap of the under wear and wherever else you could think of!), and referring to them while writing exam answers! Most students call it 'copying', while teachers prefer the term 'cheating'!

Since the time this whole Communism-education had begun, I had looked at it with healthy skepticism. Agreed that all of us had got admission to these professional courses, only thanks to some Russian zealot's belief that foreign students like us could be easily indoctrinated into Communist ideology but who would embrace Communism just by listening to high-flying concepts like 'class conflict' and 'equal distribution of public wealth'? For that matter, what was the need of making all the students watch the Communist Party's national conventions? Did someone in the Soviet think-tank really believe that such meaningless, dreary experiences generated a special affinity towards Lenin's ideology?

Then there was that dreadful thing called Scientific Communism, full of Lenin's rambling thoughts on science and some rabid red propaganda of attributing famous discoveries to various Soviet scientists. Who in their right frame of mind would simply forget names like Alexander Fleming as the discoverer of Penicillin or John Logie Baird as the inventor of television? Just because Russian textbooks claimed so, were we expected to blindly believe that some ABC-kov and XYZ-pov had achieved those feats, exactly a month or a year earlier?

The whole subject was simply disgusting!

✣

It took a Sanjay Gupta to voice our sentiments.

One day, we were walking through a corridor and Molotov was coming from the other side. Sanjay dramatically shushed us down and started talking in a conspiratorial tone.

"Shhh...quiet. Don't say anything, otherwise that grand old man will be sent to Siberia."

"What are you saying?"

"Don't you know that Molotov is now placed under strict KGB surveillance?"

"What? Why?"

"They think he is secretly planning an Anti-Communism student revolution."

"Hah! What nonsense? That poor man won't even hurt a fly."

"Yes, I know. But unfortunately he has come into the KGB eye."

"Yeah? How?"

"For years they had been wondering why the hell were these foreign students running away from Communist ideology... many investigations were carried out to find out the reasons. Then, recently one of their agents attended Molotov's lecture and found out why!"

Our laughter after this punch line was so explosive that even Molotov stopped dead in his track and looked around like a scared rabbit!

✣

Sanjay offered a study in contrasts. On one hand, he was constantly making fun of all things Communist and on the other hand, he had got selected as a guest member of *Komsomol* by topping every exam on the subject. *Komsomol* was the Soviet Communist Party's youth wing and one of its main goals was to identify and nurture young students with special fondness for Communism.

Every year, *Komsomol's* city representatives scouted for potential targets among the new college students and from our batch they had chosen Sanjay and a few more. Every weekend, such new recruits were asked to attend a special club, where they were given some topics to discuss and debate and given the privilege to mingle with the local party chiefs.

On one such weekend, Sanjay came back past midnight, dishevelled and drunk, after attending the city Communist Party chief's birthday party. Like a dutiful roommate, I made his bed, helped him change, and asked him to go to sleep. But there is something about alcohol that makes people talk incessantly and philosophically! He looked drowsy but his mind refused to relax. He just kept tossing and turning in bed, talking to himself in short muffled sentences. Lying there on my bed, I listened to his garbled words. Looking at the smoke-detector, I kept thinking about Sanjay's earlier quip that it was actually a secret camera planted by KGB! Could it be true? If it was, then Sanjay's mumblings were enough to land us both behind bars!

"Bastards, bloody bastards, all of them! Telling one thing outside and doing the opposite in their own houses...giving people sub-standard things...rationing food in the name of sharing equally... telling them to shun capitalist goods...telling them that the West is morally corrupt...just go and look into their houses...piles of latest capitalist goods from the West...all branded, expensive chocolates, cigarettes, wines, whiskies, electronics...you name it, they have it! Bastards, bloody bastards, all of them! Shouting 'Long live Lenin, Long live Communism!' Where is Lenin now? Where is communism? They are dead...long dead!"

I listened to his tirade. Though he was not in a position to talk sensibly to anyone, yet whatever he was mumbling made perfect sense to me. Be it Lincoln's equality or Lenin's—it was just a pipe dream in any corner of the world. Some people were always going to be more equal than others!

March 1986

Winds of change had started blowing. The Communist Party's General Secretary Mikhail Gorbachev and his speech at the party convention in Moscow were the only things people were talking about. The cherubic bald man in his mid-50s was fast becoming the most popular Soviet icon. He was challenging the age-old Iron Curtain diktats and speaking of things that no one had ever dared to talk about. He wanted to restructure the socio-political system. He wanted to bring more openness into its functioning. He wanted to sow the seeds of democracy. He wanted to accelerate the economy.

Prestroika...Glasnost...Demokratizatsiya...Uskoreniye.... Soviet Union was discovering new words in its lexicon and the youth was lapping it up! Perhaps a new dawn was just around the corner!

□□□

The Vanishing Act

May 19, 1986

The day had begun as usual. We were getting ready for our morning classes.

A messenger from the warden's office suddenly came and informed us, "Sanjay Gupta, your mother has come to meet you. You can wait in your room."

Sanjay's mother? Here? Why?

I looked at him questioningly. He looked equally baffled as he mumbled, "I never knew she was coming here." I indicated that I was leaving for the lecture. He acknowledged with a nervous wink.

When I left the room, I did not have a clue that that it was the last time I was seeing my best friend.

✣

I returned to our room at three in the afternoon.

Everything was quiet. As usual, Igor was not there. But strangely, even Sanjay was nowhere to be seen. His usually messy bed looked neatly done.

"The Mom Effect," I smiled to myself.

But where was he? And where was his mother? Was everything alright?

Somebody knocked on the door. Once again it was the messenger from the warden's office.

"You have been called to the warden's office."

I was suddenly very nervous as I walked out of the room.

✣

"Your roommate Sanjay Gupta has left for India. His mother had come here to take him with her. They have already left."

The warden's words did not make any sense to me. I just stared at him blankly. He continued, "His grandfather is on his deathbed. The family wants him there."

Sanjay's grandfather was 95 and had been in coma for the last two years. Then, why this sudden development? What was happening? Why did he have to leave without even meeting me?

The warden looked at me impassively. Then he took out something from his drawer. "He left for you this box of Indian sweets."

Box of sweets? Before going to see a dying grandfather? My mind was spinning. Without saying anything, I took the box and trudged back to our room.

✣

Once inside our room, I opened the box--not because I wanted to have the sweets, but because I had nothing else to do. There were just two barfis inside. But they were carefully wrapped in a parchment-like paper. I looked at the paper carefully and immediately saw it--miniscule Hindi letters. It was a message.

I took out the magnifying glass from my lab-kit. The tiny letters said, 'Communism ki kitaab...panna chautis.' So there was something on page 34 of his Communism book.

I opened Sanjay's cupboard to take out his Communism book. The cupboard was empty! Sanjay's books, his clothes, his guitar--everything was gone. It was as if all of a sudden Sanjay had simply vanished--from my room, from my life! Whatever secret he had wanted to share with me had gone with him.

✣

For almost 15 minutes I sat stunned on my bed. My head was buzzing with countless questions. Then it came to me in a flash! What if the Communism book he was talking about was not his? What if he had scribbled the message on page 34 of my Communism book?

I slowly got up from the bed and opened my study-table drawer. My Communism book was lying right on top. As I picked it up, a yellow envelope slipped out. With trembling hands I opened it. There were four hastily scribbled notebook pages with Sanjay's all-too-familiar stylish handwriting!

□□□

The letter

Dear Sada,

By the time you return from college, I will be gone. I am going back to India for good!

I know I should have waited or came there to say goodbye but I don't think I would have managed to do that with dry eyes. So skipping that ritual. Maaf karna, yaar! I have never been good at saying goodbyes.

Since you are reading this letter, it is obvious that you have cracked my hastily devised clue. I could have simply kept this letter on your table but wasn't sure whether that would be a good idea or not. Especially since what I am going to tell you is still a very hush-hush secret here. Also, that way I could test your intelligence one last time!

Ok, first things first. Let me answer the biggest question. Why?

Do you remember, just two days ago we were wondering why so many armoured trucks were offloading so many children in the hospital campus and why had the ward been cordoned off? Well, today I know the answers to these questions and that is why I am leaving.

These children have been brought from towns around Chernobyl. They are all suffering from severe radiation exposure. Remember Chernobyl, the town where they said there was a nuclear reactor accident some weeks ago? The Pravda and the state television had said that it was a minor incident, which was under investigation. But in fact, there was nothing minor about it.

Today, when my mother came to meet me, she showed me some magazine clippings, which she had carefully hidden in her suitcase in the folds of her saris. Putting a finger on her lips, she signalled me to keep quiet before giving those pages to me. Those were articles from last week's Time and Newsweek magazines and they had described Chernobyl as the worst nuclear accident till date.

Sada, Chernobyl was a disaster in the truest sense of the term. They are saying that radioactivity released from there would take almost two to three centuries to go away from that region. They are expecting thousands, if not millions, to suffer from its effects. From pneumonia and hormone disorders to cancer and congenital deformities, they are expecting the worst. And do you know what the Soviets did? They just tried to hide everything from everybody. They accepted only when the neighbouring Scandinavian scientists found out that the sudden radioactive surge in the region had origins in Chernobyl.

To say that I was shocked to learn all that would be an understatement. More than that, I was dismayed. My mother just asked me two questions--if I still thought that Communism was the path I wanted to take up and why Soviet Union was hiding the Chernobyl truth from the world and more importantly, from its own people.

I had no answers.

She had always been against my decision to come here. All her life, she had seen her father, a staunch Communist leader, work tirelessly with one blind zealot belief. She had hated Communism simply because it had taken her father away from her mother and her. She was really disappointed when I told her of my decision to come to Russia to learn Medicine and see the bedrock of Communism from up close. Like all good mothers, she too had finally given into my wishes but now she said that she had had enough of my Communism fascination and that she was here to take me back to India as she did not want to see me die from cancer five years down the line.

I must say that in one way, I was relieved that she was taking this decision for me. More than Medicine, it was Communism that had drawn me here. I had always been fascinated by my grandfather's passion. I had nurtured dreams of becoming a political leader like him. But disillusionment was already beginning to set in. Molotov's lectures, Komsomol meetings...what I had seen here was already making me question my decision and Chernobyl was the final tipping point.

I lost my father very early in life. It was my mother, who looked after me with help from my grandfather. Now that grandfather is lying in bed in a vegetable state, my mother wants me to go back with her to look after our family farms. Though her teary pleas did play an important role, the primary reason is my own disillusionment. I know that the Chernobyl radiation may not affect us here, but what about those thousands in the vicinity, who were exposed and were given no warning for days? Did Lenin want this?

Ok, enough of this rambling. My mother is imploring me not to leave anything behind but I wanted to tell you everything before I left. What I will do in future, I haven't yet decided. But I am sure it will be something miles away from both Medicine as well as Communism, or for that matter, politics of any kind.

You have been an excellent friend. I will never forget you. Don't let my decision affect you. I am sure you will make a fine doctor.

All the best.

And yes, please tear off this letter and flush it away immediately. I don't want you to get into any trouble.

Sanjay
*PS: If you ever want to do something for me, just do one thing. When Molotov turns his back to write some Commie stuff on the blackboard, say 'F*** O**'loudly! Just kidding!*

Wiping away my tears, I smiled.

It was the first major jolt to my Russian medical ambitions, one that made me think long and hard about my future. But I was determined not to lose focus. I was determined not to end up as yet another meaningless casualty of the Chernobyl tragedy.

Come what may, Sadanand Borkar was going to become a doctor!

□□□

Vacations

July 8, 1990

Edberg tosses the ball high over his head...arches his body and serves. A perfect serve...kicking high and aiming into Becker's mid-riff...the German awkwardly fends it off. The handsome Swede is already raising his arms in triumph as the returned ball loops high and lands outside the line. Game, set, and match and the Wimbledon championship to Stefan Edberg! After five hard-fought sets of exceptional serve-and-volley tennis, the champ holds the glittering trophy aloft! The crowd cheers with a deafening applause.

The memorable TV images of the Wimbledon final as usual kick-started my vacation. It was almost like a ritual. I would finish my exams by the first week of July and leave for Mumbai. Shaking off the jet lag, I would sit in front of the TV, intently watching the Wimbledon final, taking in every small detail. The faded green lawns, the Rolex scoreboard, the buzz in the crowd, the umpire's authoritative announcements, the ballboys' alacrity and of course, the genius of the players. It was all so fascinating.

But most importantly the match gave me some time to come to terms with my life back home. It was so convenient to just sit transfixed in front of the TV without having to answer anybody's awkward questions about my present or future. Even if some potentially difficult discussion ever began, I could always veer the conversation towards the intricacies of tennis!

This was my fourth visit home in the five years that I had spent in Russia. The first two vacations had been good, even great at times. Then I used to enjoy coming back to my roots--being in familiar places, interacting with familiar people--but as years progressed, things started to change.

Most of my school friends had moved to different places to pursue their careers. I practically had no contact with them. My family and my relatives were still going around in the never-ending circle of births, deaths, engagements, marriages, naming ceremonies, and thread ceremonies but the geographical distance between me and them had stripped me off any feelings for those rituals. The places and the faces started to become more and more unfamiliar. The interactions started to become dreaded chores of monosyllabic greetings and small talk. I felt as if I had nothing in common with them. Their world, their priorities, their feelings, even their language--everything felt so distant, so alien.

The roots had started to loosen!

In Russia I was a free bird, a carefree young man, who did anything and everything as he pleased. It was this sense of freedom that was going to tear me away from my own family. The moment I landed in India, I felt caged. I felt as if everyone around me was watching me closely, as if I was some interesting specimen. I had begun to hate every moment of my time in India; I just longed to go back to Russia.

Father and I--now, that had always been a difficult equation, even in the best of times, even before going to Russia. I had always had problems adjusting to his ultra-cautious, ultra-conservative, and ultra-authoritarian attitude but now I just could not tolerate any of his comments and suggestions. Every casual comment seemed to me like criticism and every simple suggestion seemed like an order! I couldn't even talk to him for two minutes without getting into an argument.

My mother brought a new set of problems. She was constantly nagging me to get married. Yielding to her wish, I had even gone to the extent of 'seeing' a few girls–a peculiar Indian custom, where the potential bride was paraded in front of the potential bridegroom! But after meeting those Russian girls, these Indian ones seemed too tame for my liking. Finally, after going through three harrowing 'girl-seeing' experiences, I decided that it was time to put my foot down and make it very clear that I had no intention of marrying so soon. I got my chance soon enough!

"Sada, what are you doing tomorrow evening?" As usual, my mother broached the subject in a round-about manner.

"Nothing in particular, Mom," I informed.

She excitedly said, "Oh, that's good. I have called my friend Shalu and her family for tea. Remember Shalini-aunty, who used to stay at Bhandup?"

"Who? The one who used to wear golden specs and had a weird set of teeth?" I asked with a worried expression.

Mom continued happily, "Oh, so you do remember her. Yes, that's the one. Now she has moved to a bigger flat in Andheri and runs her own fashion boutique."

"So, why is she coming here? To meet you? Isn't that strange? I don't think I have seen her in the last 10 years." I wondered aloud.

"Well, actually she is coming to see you," mother finally let the cat out of the bag.

"Me? Why?" I asked exasperatedly.

Her awkward silence gave me the clue. "Oh, Mom, not again! I do not have any intention of marrying her daughter."

"Babu, why are you so negative? What is the harm in just 'seeing' her? Take your time. They have only one daughter and they have made some good provisions for her!" (The only times mother called me 'Babu' were when she wanted me to do something against my wish!)

From the bedroom came the sound of my sister's shrill laughter. I could almost visualize Deepti's contorted face. I suddenly lost it.

I shouted, “Why are you so obsessed with marriage, Mom? Isn’t it enough that you and father have ruined Deepti’s life? What was it that you were saying before marrying her off? That she will improve, she will be very happy. Now that’s one happy daughter laughing like a wailing banshee! Do you want me to end up like her?”

One look at my mother and I remembered that old saying about spoken words and arrows—once shot can never be retrieved. Mother’s face had turned grey. Her lips were quivering. Her eyes were filled with tears. She just turned away and steadied herself against the wall.

Hearing my outburst, father had walked into the hall. He too looked shaken to the core. His eyes too were filled to the brim. Looking straight into my eyes, he said, “Sada, from now on no one in the family will tell you to get married. It will be entirely your decision.”

Then he slowly went back to the bedroom where my schizophrenic sister was laughing hysterically!

□□□

A story to forget

That night our house was unusually quiet. After that outburst, none of us had said a word. We even had dinner separately and in total silence. I lay down on the sofa-cum-bed in the hall. Mom and dad had retired to the bedroom. I just kept tossing and turning all night long. Something was weighing heavily on everyone's conscience, especially mine.

The only person who was sleeping without a care in the world was my sister. Lying on her bed on the floor in my parents' room, she slept like a child. Whatever demons resided in her split mind had been stilled for the moment. She had been heavily sedated.

✣

How does a person who has lived a perfectly normal and fruitful life for almost 21 years, suddenly develop a split personality?

I had never come to terms with the psychiatrist's answer, when he had dispassionately told me, "It happens!"

How can it just happen? That too, to Deepti, my dear sister!

Deepti was four years older to me. She had always been bright in academics, a topper in her school. As a person, she was a loner. A shy girl, she seldom said anything more than what was absolutely necessary. The only time she would let go of her inhibitions was in my company. Together we had played so many pranks on different friends of hers and mine.

The problem had started after her class XII, when she could not get admission to Medicine, missing out by a few marks. For two months, she barely spoke to anyone. All of us tried to cheer her up but she just refused to come out of that state of shock. We thought, "So what? So many students fail to get into Medicine. They get depressed for a while and then move on with life."

Deepti too moved on with life. She enrolled for BSc but something was amiss. There was a strange listlessness in her. Not only had she cut herself off from her friends, she had also distanced herself from us. For days together she would not go to college, saying that she was too tired! She cleared the papers with reasonably good marks every year but her heart was not in it.

When I was trying to fight off my class XII debacle, she passed BSc and joined a small company in a clerical position. My struggle to get into Medical had made her even more reticent. We were no longer close emotionally; as it is she had stopped confiding me long before that. Then I got my Russian break and left. Looking back, I still remember that strange glint of resentment in her eyes the night I first announced my decision to go to Russia. She had never said anything directly to me about my plans. It was as if she was angry with me for leaving her behind! I was indeed going to leave her behind—far, far behind!

✣

March 1988. It was my third year in Russia.

The hostel's peon had come to my room to tell me that I had a call from my mother. A phone from home was a rarity and I ran downstairs anxiously.

"Sada, I have something to tell you."My mother's sombre tone chilled my blood. Was everything alright? Had someone passed away?

"Last night Deepti was hospitalised."

"W-what? What happened?"

"She slashed her wrists."

"What? Why?"

"We don't know. The last few days she had been acting quite strangely. She had left her job and started staying at home. She would tear off her clothes, abuse us, throw things at us...we kept her at home thinking she would eventually come to her senses but she turned more and more violent and then, when I was busy cooking, she slashed her wrists with the kitchen knife!"

"How is she now?"

"She is okay now. But the doctors say she has a mental disorder."

"Mental disorder? What disorder?"

"They say she has a split personality. Schizophrenia. They say she will continue having such attacks unless she is put on long-term medication."

"So?"

"What do you mean by 'so'?"

"Mom, there is nothing wrong in giving her medicines if experts have prescribed them. What is your problem?"

"I don't want to give her any long-term medicine. She is just under stress. I don't believe this split personality stuff. My daughter is not mad!"

"Mom, you can be so adamant sometimes. How is Father? What does he say?"

"Your father and I feel the same way. We have decided to take another opinion."

I hung up. My elder sister had just been diagnosed with Split Personality Disorder and my parents were refusing to believe that diagnosis and I was just dumbly, numbly standing thousands of miles away in a far-off country!

What followed was a series of unfortunate events. My parents did everything that should not have been done. They refused to believe any of the psychiatrists, even after at least a dozen had confirmed the diagnosis. They placed their faith in alternative therapies--homeopathy, naturopathy, electrotherapy, magnetotherapy...every possible 'pathy' and therapy was unleashed on poor Deepti. Simultaneously, they were also consulting *gurus* and *babas* for religious and supernatural therapies. It was easy for them to believe that 'someone has cast an evil eye on her' and 'the current planetary alignment has conspired against her' but impossible to come to terms with the diagnosis of a psychiatric illness. Out of that peculiar mindset they arrived at the worst decision possible. They decided to marry her off!

Once again I received a call. I was then preparing for my third year exams. Once again, I walked to the phone-desk with trepidation. Mother was on the line.

"Sada, Deepti is getting married in a temple tomorrow."

"What? Deepti is getting married! Why?"

"It will be a small, simple ceremony. We have only called a few close relatives."

"Are you out of your mind? How can you marry her off? Is she better?"

"Yes, she is much better now. She has even started working part-time in a nearby lawyer's office. Baba has told us that she just needs to get married to get these things out of her head. He told us that once the first child is born, she will be completely okay.'"

"Now which *baba* you are talking about? That Nityanand Baba?"

"No, that fellow was a fraud. This one is a genuine one--Ramsagar Baba. He has his *ashram* in Borivali and has cured hundreds of such cases."

"But what's the rush? My vacation will be starting soon...why can't you postpone it till then?"

"No, Baba has said that tomorrow is the best *muhurat*, most auspicious according to Deepti's *kundali*. If we miss this, then we will have to wait for 10 months."

"Who is the groom?"

"He is also a disciple of Baba...works as a teacher and stays in Andheri."

"Have you met him or his family?"

"Yes, they are nice people. Very understanding. Their own daughter was also suffering from something similar but was cured by Baba. They have promised to keep Deepti happy."

"What about Deepti? Is she ready?"

"Oh, you know how girls are. She was crying the whole day. She kept saying that she does not want to leave us and that she would marry only if you attend the wedding, but then we made her understand. Now she is okay."

"Okay, Mom. Give her my best wishes. Tell her I love her! Tell her I...I..." I couldn't complete the sentence. I just hung up.

My eyes were smarting with tears. My sister was getting married and where was I!

✣

Baba's assurances had not worked. The husband was an alcoholic and worse still, a wife-beater. Within three months Deepti had fled from that house to return home. Within the next three months, a mutually consented divorce deal was worked out. Marriage had done one thing for Deepti--it had given her a split marriage to go with her split mind!

When I arrived for my vacation that year, I finally convinced my parents to accept that Deepti was a psychiatric patient, who needed proper evaluation and treatment from qualified doctors. She was put on medication. The road was not easy. Her disease was a frustrating up-and-down affair. Sometimes for months, she would be almost normal, even be able to take up small part-time jobs and then out of the blue, her violent behaviour would resurface.

One psychiatrist was candid enough to tell us that it would be a lifelong affair. When he was telling this in his clipped clinical voice, Deepti was in one of her vacant spells, lost in some far away world seen only through her eyes; my parents were looking devastated and old; and I was just thinking of booking an early ticket to Russia.

✣

That was way back in 1988 and now we were in 1990.So little had changed in between for the four of us. Deepti was still in her own far-off world; mother and father still looked devastated and old (much more now than then!) and, tossing on my bed, once again I was thinking of advancing the date of my ticket to Russia.

Vacations to India were not fun anymore!

□□□

My first case

"Okay, let's move on to Room No.17. Here is a classic case of alcoholic cirrhosis where you can see every possible sign of chronic liver failure. All of you can take a quick look at this. Sadanand, prepare this case for presentation. We will have a detailed discussion tomorrow."

When our General Medicine professor Dr Anatoly Khruschev uttered these words, a strange sense of excitement and nervousness crept into me. It was going to be my first case presentation, my first real introduction to the field of medicine.

It was seven in the evening when I came back to the ward. In the meantime, I had devoured the textbook and mugged everything about cirrhosis and liver failure. It all seemed so straightforward. Just go there, take a detailed history, make a careful examination, note down everything, and then present those findings in front of the group. I had it all covered.

I first approached the staff-in-charge nurse. "Sister, I want to examine Room No. 17. Tomorrow, I have to present that case."

The sister-in-charge was busy writing something. She looked at me wearily.

"Are you sure?"

"Yes, Sister. Why do you ask?"

"Why? Because that poor man has been 'presented' 10 times in the last three months. He is sick and tired and about to die, and still the 'show' continues!"

I didn't know what to say. I looked at her, puzzled.

She shrugged and said, "Okay, what's new? Go ahead. Have

your fill. Just make sure that you don't make him angry. He almost went for the throat of the last student!"

As I approached Room No.17, I was no longer sure that it was going to be as straightforward as I had thought.

When I reached Room No.17, it was empty. The patient had gone to the toilet. But within seconds, even before I could go through his charts, he came back, and lay down. Lying there, he looked like a skeleton--a skeleton with a feeding tube in the nose, an IV-line in the hand and a catheter in the bladder; a skeleton with deep yellow eyes, bloated tummy, and scratched and bruised skin!

I introduced myself and said, "Do you mind if I ask you a few questions and then examine you?"

He hardly had any strength to speak but still managed to speak in a deep hoarse voice. "One more medical student, huh? Who are you? An Indian? I like Indians, they are nice people. Polite and respectful. Okay, go ahead. Ask me what you want."

But when I started asking him questions according to the textbook's history-taking scheme, he began to get irritated. Summoning all his strength, he admonished, "Hey, stop. Stop right there. No more silly questions. When did it start, how did it start, how did it progress...can't you ask anything else? Do you know my name? Have you thought of asking me that? Or asking me about how I lived and what do I think about my past, present, and future? I am not Room No.17. I am Vassily Ivankov. Vroom VroomVassily."

After that he just kept talking and I listened patiently.

"I used to be an athlete...a 100 metres dash champion...the fastest man in Soviet Union. Girls swooned over me. Boys looked up to me as a role model. I was the Vroom Vroom Vassily, who ran like the wind. I broke all records, won dozens of medals and led a great life. Then, just as I was preparing for my Olympic trials,

I had a car accident. I broke both my legs...stayed in plaster for weeks and when I recovered, my world had changed. No longer was I the fastest; my competitors who once quaked and quivered in my presence, now left me far behind. I lost the chance to go for the Olympics as well as the cause that kept me focused and motivated. I married and tried to settle down. But domesticity was not for me. I was wired differently. The result was for all to see. After years of bitter bickering, I separated from my wife and two sons."

"We Russians are fond of our Vodka and finally Vodka became my only soulmate, the one who understood all my sorrows and helped me drown them. Years passed. But soulmates too extract their price in full and I had to pay mine. Now I know I don't have much time...but hey, I don't care. For me, my life had ended when I ceased to be Vroom VroomVassily. The rest was just living for the sake of living. Now, here I am. A battered, bruised skeleton!"

"Six months ago, I was admitted in this hospital by my landlord, who was looking after me for all these years. You know why? Because he was my biggest fan! He could not bear to watch me wither away and die. In the first month, my two sons came to meet me. I saw them after many years. They are now young men, strong like oxen but empty in their heads. They told me how much they hated me for abandoning them and their mother. They told me how their mother had worked hard to raise them and how she loathed me every waking moment. They told me that they had come to see me one last time to feel good about my misery. They also told me that they would not be coming for my funeral. They perhaps expected me to break down and plead for forgiveness but listening to their outbursts, I felt nothing inside. To me, they looked like two melodramatic buffoons trying to evoke sympathy. Life does such strange things to you. The people whom you once called your own become perfect strangers and perfect strangers go on to become your best mates."

"Now the nurses and doctors here push, poke and prod, and needlessly try to keep me alive. Medical students come in hordes and look at me wide-eyed as an interesting specimen. And I keep looking at everything as if I am watching a never-ending third-rate film."

While listening to his monologue, I began to wonder how he had suddenly found the energy to deliver such a long speech. As he paused wearily, I decided to make my move.

I softly asked, "If you don't mind, may I at least examine you?"

Visibly tired from his long speech, he just nodded.

I started examining his disease-ravaged body. Sparse hair, bruises, scratch marks, muscle wasting, deep jaundice, ascites, spider nevi, hard granular-feeling liver....I was noting my observations, when he suddenly he grabbed my hand and sat up. Before I could even ask him what was wrong, he slumped forward and vomited violently over me. It was no ordinary vomiting. It was hematemesis. I was drenched in bright red, fresh blood.

Shaken and terrified, I looked at the man slumped in my arms. He had turned grey and had stopped breathing.

I shrieked, "Sister!"

✣

My first case presentation never took place. Vroom Vroom Vassily died. The death certificate mentioned the cause of death as 'Alcoholic Cirrhosis with Hepatic Failure'.

It failed to mention that he died in my arms! My first case taught me more about Medicine than many others that followed in its wake.

□□□

The Speech

December, 25 1991

The world was celebrating Christmas but in Russia, where they followed the Orthodox Church, it was still two weeks away. The day had passed uneventfully. I was just about to finish dinner, when a junior, Rahul Subramanian, came running into the dining hall. Through his thick spectacles, his big, bulging eyes were looking as if they would pop out any moment.

Breathlessly he sputtered, "Hey, what are you guys doing here? Come, everyone is in the TV room. Gorbachev is going to make an important speech. It must be something really serious since they are announcing the same thing over and over again, both on TV and radio."

What now? We looked at each other in exasperation. It was a difficult time to be in Soviet Union. From the time I had returned from my vacation, the entire country had seemed like a volcano that was about to erupt. The August Coup against Gorbachev and Boris Yeltsin's valiant response to it had dramatically changed the political power equations. Gorbachev, the President of the Soviet Union, was rapidly losing ground. Yeltsin, the Russian Prime Minister, was being looked at as the man of the moment. Of course, nobody was talking about it openly but the general mood was quite palpable.

So, was this the end of the road for Gorby? Were we now going to see Yeltsin become the new president of Soviet Union?

What changes was he going to bring in? With innumerable uncomfortable questions on our minds, we rushed to the TV room.

There was an uneasy silence in the crammed TV room when Gorbachev first appeared. It was clear that this time around, there was not going to be any spontaneous applause, the likes of which he had routinely received in his heyday TV appearances.

His famous bald head with its distinctive port wine stain still looked very much the same. But the face looked very different. There was no smile. It looked careworn and haggard. Sitting with drooping shoulders, he first made sure that the camera was about to roll. Then, with a solemn expression and a heavy voice that barely concealed his sadness, he began.

"Dear compatriots and fellow citizens, as a result of the newly formed situation, the creation of the Commonwealth of Independent States, I hereby discontinue my activities as the USSR President."

Wasn't it expected? But still it felt like a sharp stab in the heart. Wasn't this the same man whom, not so long ago, we had wholeheartedly cheered on as the saviour of this nation? Wasn't this the same man, who was supposed to change this iron-curtained country for the better?

Gorby rambled on about how it was important to bring about changes in the shackled system and what previously untenable things his policies had managed to achieve. Freedom of press, freedom of religion, multi-party electoral system, reducing nuclear threat...but what would he gain by listing these so-called achievements when finally everything had come to naught?

Then he went on to say things that no one was expecting--things, which seemed too farfetched and unreal...that it was the end of the Soviet Union...about the chaos and disorder which were now unavoidable.

Was he out of his mind? Or was he telling the ugly truth? We listened with rapt attention.

"......The old system collapsed before the new one had time to begin working, and the crisis in the society became even more acute. The most damaging thing about this crisis is the breakup of the statehood.

And today I am worried by our people's loss of the citizenship of a great country. The consequences may turn out to be very hard for everyone.

I am leaving my post with apprehension, but also with hope, with faith in you, your wisdom and force of spirit. We are the heirs of a great civilization, and its rebirth into a new, modern and dignified life now depends on one and all."

There was a stunned silence in the TV room after he concluded his speech.

Gorbachev resigning as the president was one thing but a total collapse of the Soviet Union was quite another. People come and go but an entire country vanishing into thin air just like that? And that too, the country, which was the second superpower in the world!

No one knew what was happening. No one knew what was going to happen. No one said anything to each other. No one had anything to say to each other. With their own individual sets of anxious questions on their minds, everyone quietly dispersed and went to their rooms.

Gorbachev had not just delivered a resignation speech. He had delivered a funeral speech. Soviet Union was dead!

The future looked bleak. Very bleak.

□□□

Russian Dollars

April 1992

"Doctor, Code Red."

I woke up with a start. Rubbing my eyes I looked at the clock. 1:45 am. Shit! Not even 15 minutes of sleep! Clinical rotation in the Accident-Emergency department was the worst. As final year medical students, we were the typical unpaid clerks-cum-ward-boys with no powers. We were supposed to witness the actual 'action' from afar but were the first ones called on the scene to fill up the history-examination-investigation forms and do all sorts of sundry menial jobs.

I walked sleepily to the emergency room. The nursing staff-in-charge, Lydia, was standing all alone with a long face outside a curtained cubicle.

"What happened?" I asked.

True to her style, Lydia came straight to the point. "You have to fill the DC."

My lethargy vanished. Surprised, I asked, "Death certificate? What happened? And why is there no resuscitation team?"

"What's the use of a resuscitation team in a DOA?"

"Dead on arrival? How?"

"What else? Suicide! This is the fifth case in three days. An old pensioner--brought here stone dead. Found in a bathtub with a slashed wrist."

"Any idea why he killed himself?"

Lydia did not mince words. "What is there to live for in this country anymore? Depression and despair everywhere! The people who brought him here said that one week back he had lost his wife in our hospital. They said that she had had pneumonia but the required antibiotics were out of stock! Since that day, he had been drinking heavily and had stopped talking with anybody."

An uneasy silence hung between us for a minute. Then I said, "Sister Lydia, if you don't mind, can I ask you something else?"

"Don't worry. Go ahead. *Glasnost. Perestroika.* It's a free country now." She replied with a cynical laugh.

I hesitantly ventured ahead. "They told me that your husband could exchange my rubles for dollars. Is it true?"

Lydia's cynical laugh was back. "Yes, it is true. He has some business friends in Poland, from where he gets his dollars. Anyway, the way the ruble is falling everyday, soon all our savings will vanish unless we hoard some dollars. Is there any use of these rubles now? You now need a bagful of them to buy a handful of groceries. Russia running on dollars--would anybody have imagined such a thing? But that is how it is and that is how it is going to be. No one trusts the ruble anymore. They are just useless printed notes now. In villages, people have already gone back to the barter system. Give potatoes, take chicken. Give chicken, take vodka. Give vodka, take anything! That is what is happening. The only hard currency is dollar. How much do you need?"

My cautious middle-class upbringing made me ask her. "Will there be any problem? Is it legal?"

Suddenly Lydia became serious. With a lost look, she said, "Legal or illegal, who cares about it now? The ones, who were making the laws, broke this country into pieces. Now it is the law of the jungle. Everyone has to fend for himself. My Yuri was once the member of the village council. Now he sells dollars in the black market. So, does that mean we are thieves? Or does it mean that we don't love our country? No. We are just trying to stay afloat. Survival--that's the name of the game today."

Suddenly, recovering her poise, she said, "Oh, forget that. How many dollars do you want?"

"Err...Is it possible to get 50?"

She laughed and said, “For that you don’t need Yuri’s help. I must be having that much in my purse.”

As she handed me five brand new $10 bills, she pointed at the curtained cubicle with her eyes and said, “Don’t forget to fill the DC for the DOA.”

I nodded sheepishly.

✣

It was 10 am when I finally managed to go off duty. As I walked out of the hospital, I saw the old ladies, the babushkas, setting up their roadside stalls. Gone were the days when they used to sell homemade pickles and jams for a few kopeks; now they traded all things foreign--cigarette packs, chocolate bars, cola cans. All top Western brands!

I picked up a Mars bar and asked, “How much?”

Without even looking at me, the babushka replied, “That will be one dollar!”

We were now living in a different Russia! Russia that ran on dollars; Russia that ran after dollars!

□□□

Rasskazov

'Dr Rasskazov, Doctor of Medical Sciences, Professor Academician, Head of Surgery.'

The shining brass nameplate on the door was my first introduction to this supposedly eccentric genius. But when he actually turned up for our class, the first impression was rather disappointing. A short man of sallow complexion, sparse hair and a beaky nose, Rasskazov had a nasal feminine voice. Even when he spoke normally it always seemed as if he was shouting to make his point.

Whatever may have been his less than impressive physical attributes, Rasskazov was a legend in our college corridors. He was the member of the special medical team, which treated all foreign and Russian dignitaries. His knife had traversed far and deep into many a president and prime minister's innards. It was rumoured that an ex-Soviet Premier had gifted him a huge dacha (a villa) after the surgeon had removed a cancerous growth from his intestines. Obviously, his close connections within Moscow's power corridors meant that he was constantly busy attending to the aches, pains, and swellings of some minister's wife or some politician's nephew. That also meant that he did not have enough time to teach us.

The typical Rasskazov class went somewhat like this. Our group of 12 students would arrive at the classroom at 8:30 am. "What's today's topic?' someone would enquire. "Intestinal obstruction," someone would answer. Then we would wait and wait and wait for the next three hours. If we were lucky, then the man would make an appearance in the dying minutes of the three-hour-long session--always irritable; always in a hurry; always with something else on his mind.

His method of teaching was horrible to say the least. He just did not know how to simplify things; in fact he loved to complicate the simplest of things. But his idea about the study of surgery was rather simple. He expected every student to mug up 'Surgery by Rasskazov', his 1000-page book, which was half-filled with pointless, flowery quotes by Lenin, Pushkin, Gorky and Tolstoy. If you could do that, you were a clever student. If you could not, you were in serious trouble!

✣

Midway through my final year I already knew that I was in serious trouble. I tried hard to concentrate on his book but in vain. In plain words, "It was bloody bullshit!"Don't you believe me? Let me give you an example.

"Try as you may, you won't hear a sound. Everything seems still and silent. Like the broken bell of a deserted church. Or better still, the deathly silence in a graveyard on a no-moon night."

Well, this is how Rasskazov's book described the signs of Paralytic Ileus, a type of intestinal obstruction! His way of writing was not only pretentious and phony, but also insipid and uninteresting. With his crazy literary excesses, Rasskazov just made me doubly sure that I abhorred surgery!

The interminable wait for him in the lecture hall was equally irritating. Out of our group of 12, only Studious Susanne and Dorky Dave used to religiously wait for him till the end. Very often the rest of us would make ourselves scarce after waiting for two hours. It was impossible that the hawk-eyed Rasskazov would not notice that and when he did, he promptly issued a warning. Characteristically, he excused the Russians from the group and just targeted me and Akhilesh Sinha, my Bihari partner.

"You are not attending my classes. You are not doing well in the exams. Better behave or face the consequences." He shouted in his squeaky girly voice.

Standing in front of him, we tried to defend ourselves. "But Sir, we do come to class. We leave only after waiting for you for more than two hours and that too, we go to the library to study."

Rasskazov's squeakiness rose a few decibels. "Oh, so you are now trying to blame me for not attending the classes? You bloody Indians. You have always been cheaters."

That racist remark suddenly sparked off an altercation. My firebrand Bihari partner, who had once been suspended for breaking someone's nose in a brawl, hurled at Rasskazov some of the choicest Hindi expletives. Akhilesh almost made a move to grab the professor by the collar. Stunned by his move, I instinctively tried to intervene but it went horribly wrong. The next moment, both of us lost balance and landed on the floor with a thud. To top it all, as a desperate measure of a falling man, I grabbed Rasskazov's leg and like a wrestler going down in a bout, the professor crashed on top of us!

When we all disentangled ourselves and got up from the floor, Rasskazov's eyes were spouting fire. Looking at us he hissed, "You...you...I will show you what I can do!"

Akhilesh returned his stare with an equally defiant one but I was totally stunned by this unexpected turn of events. I wished I could simply disappear!

The only reason we did not get rustication orders was because of Sinha's well-connected father. It was rumoured that his father was a powerful druglord, who had every political leader in Bihar in his pocket! So obviously the wheels had turned within the wheels and someone higher up had convinced the angry professor that there were other easier ways of getting revenge!

My final exams for General Medicine, Gynaecology, ENT and Opthalmology had gone well. All the professors had already indicated that I had done well enough to pass. So, it was only Surgery that now remained between the coveted MD degree and me. It was my final frontier and to conquer that I had to win over Rasskazov! Inside my heart I knew I was doomed!

Doomsday began rather well for me. I was given a case of Cholecystitis or Gall Bladder inflammation as my major case for the exam. I was happy. I knew the topic well. The patient was cooperative and even the signs and symptoms were straightforward. I prepared the history well, wrote down my findings and rehearsed the theory in my mind. I felt confident.

"Next," the attendant called and I made my move towards the examiner's room. Rasskazov was sitting there with Dr Olga, a pleasant looking lady professor, who was known to be lenient. I rattled the history in a seasoned manner. Olga was looking suitably impressed. Rasskazov sat motionless and blank. Suddenly he said, "Okay, so you say this is a case of cholecystitis. How would you examine the patient?"

I started answering, "Sir, I would first like to inspect the affected area, then palpate it, then do the percussion and finally auscultation."

Olga nodded in agreement.

Rasskazov just snorted derisively. "So, you want to become a doctor, huh? Has Your Excellency ever cared to go through my book on surgery?" I meekly nodded. My knees felt weak. Cold sweat broke out on the back of my neck. Rasskazov continued, "How can you do palpation before percussion and auscultation? I have proved in my book that what the rest of the world says is wrong. You have to first finish percussion and auscultation and only then proceed to palpation. I am sorry I cannot let such a dull student go further. Your exam is over. You will be repeating the course for one more year."

It was difficult to say who was more shocked–me or Olga. But both of us knew one thing for sure, Rasskazov meant every word that he just had said. Olga tried to intervene, "But Dr Rasskazov..." but he just summarily dismissed her. "Please Dr Olga, do not interfere. I know this student well. He is irregular, disrespectful and ill-prepared. I am not going to let him go any further."

Down in the dumps, I tried to reason, "Sir, how can you not let me take the rest of the exam? I have studied well." He looked at me maliciously and said, "I know that. I know that. But you are still not going to pass! I am failing you in the major case and without that you cannot attempt the next cases! The game is over Indian boy!"

So that was that. My game was over.

Rasskazov had got his revenge!

□□□

Operation Surgery

Failure is a strange phenomenon. First you feel hopeless about the whole situation but after some time, you start devising strategies to overcome it. It is just like being thrown into the deep end of the pool. First you feel as though nothing can save you from sinking to the bottom, then survival instinct kicks in and you start working your legs and hands to push yourself up. My failure in Surgery induced the same response. The initial despair gave way to finding ways to 'modify' the result.

At the height of Communist reign, such a thought would have been unthinkable. But with dissolution of Communism, such things were indeed possible. I just needed the right contact. The results had not been announced officially and I had a few days to work out some strategy. The only way to overturn Rasskazov's verdict was to find someone higher up in the college hierarchy who could 'persuade' the maverick professor to change his mind. The method of persuasion was simple. The ruble was dead and the dollar was the new king. Stuff their mouths with dollars and get the result you want. That was now an open secret in the Russian examination system.

I approached Sasha, a Russian friend, who was very conversant with this.

"Bloody Rasskazov? That's a tough nut to crack."

Even Sasha's initial knee-jerk response told me how difficult that whole 'Operation Result Modification' was going to be. But then he said, "No worries. I know the rector well. He can pull you through by convincing the prof. But it will be a costly affair."

"How much?" I asked.

He named the price. "At least $2000."

I almost choked on that figure. How the hell was I ever going to raise $2000? I knew that in the black market that amount was almost close to hundred thousand rubles.

Sasha realised my problem. He had always been a nice guy, despite whatever he did outside the college campus. He said, "Okay, don't worry. I will pay for you. But you will have to pay me back after two months."

I did some quick calculations in my mind and asked, "Is it okay if I pay after three months?"

He smiled. The deal was on!

✣

True to his word, the very next day Sasha took me to the rector's room. As usual, the rector was yet to come out of his hangover. But he became alert as soon as Sasha advanced the envelope. He listened carefully to my predicament and grunted. "That Rasskazov! I just don't know how to deal with him. But don't worry. I will handle him. When is your result due?"

I mumbled. "After five days." And that was that.

When we walked out of the rector's office, I hugged Sasha. "You saved my life, buddy. I don't know what I would have told my parents if I had failed!"

He just accepted my gratitude with another of his winning smiles.

It was the time to start packing to go home. The hostel ambience was cheerful but it was also becoming quite sentimental. In the last eight years, I had made so many friends from across the world. Soon everyone would be going away--each back into his own world. Bidding adieu to friends and taking their contact details was an exercise tinged with sadness.

The day of the results arrived. All of us congregated around the college's central notice board. The college peon brought the result sheet and stuck it on the board. I was at the back of the group. Trying to make my way through that rush, I reached in front of the notice board within a few minutes. Going through the list was a breeze. My eyes rested on my name.

One word sealed my fate. 'Fail'!

Then everything went blank!

□□□

Worsening blues

So, the bribe had not worked! Even thieves have a code of honour but these medical college professors did not seem to have any! Both bastards, the rector and Rasskazov, had taken the money and had done nothing. Thanks to them, I had lost an academic year, I would have to reappear for my Surgery exam the next year, and to boost it I had incurred a debt of $2000. What would I tell my parents? How was I going to spend the next year without a hostel or any money? How was I ever going to come out of my debt? Every thought, every question felt like a sharp stab in the heart.

One by one, my classmates left the hostel, leaving to wallow in my misery. Only three students had failed in our class. Everyone knew my reason and was sympathetic, but their kind words of support did not help. Instead, they just served to repeatedly remind me of my failure.

For the first two days, I tried everything I could think of to get out of my depression...I drank, I slept, I cried, I shouted. But the dull ache inside refused to go away. Suicide? Was that the solution? I sat in the toilet for hours, holding the razor blade in my hand. Gathering courage for that extreme step seemed to be beyond me. When I finally emerged out of that toilet door, I felt like a failure in every respect!

✣

Knocks on my door...once again! Like so many times in the past, this time too the heavy thuds on my door woke me up with a start. Groggily, I opened the door. Two burly, menacing-looking baldies were standing there. From behind them, emerged Sasha. He looked embarrassed and anxious.

He mumbled, "Hi buddy, how are you doing?"

I looked at him blankly.

He continued mumbling, "Sorry to bother you at this moment but...remember, I had told you that you could return the $2000 in three months, but my friends here, from whom I had taken that money, are now demanding it within two months. Is it okay with you?"

Was it okay with me? I started laughing hysterically! Not a sarcastic, cynical laughter but a genuine happy laughter! Whatever could go wrong was going wrong, and yet I was actually feeling high. Sasha and his 'friends' started looking at me as if I had completely lost it. The scornful expression on those bullies' faces had given way to surprise and discomfort.

Sasha asked, "Are you okay? You know these things are not in my hand. If I had a choice...."

I stopped him midway through his sentence and said, "Don't worry, Sasha. I am okay. I know you tried your best to help me. Look, as it is I have no classes to attend this year. I just have to study one subject. So, instead of wasting my time crying over spilt milk, I might as well keep myself busy earning some money. Tell your friends that I will return the money within two months. Now if you please..."

I slammed the door shut!

□□□

Off to London

My bravado left me as soon as I closed that door. What was happening to me? One minute I was feeling sky-high and the next moment I was down in the dumps again. How the hell was I going to get $2000 in two months? There was no job in Russia, which would pay me that much, unless of course I decided to move to the 'dark' side and join the burgeoning Russian mafia. I did not want to do that or rather I was too afraid to do that. The middle-class Konkani mentality was still very much a part of me. It would not let me go of my 'good and respectful' side. The only option left was London. Yes, London it had to be!

Over the years, working in London had been a favourite vacation-job for most foreign students studying in Russia. I had already done that twice and had earned quite handsomely. The memories came rushing to my mind. The serpentine queues in front of the UK Consulate; the long overnight vigils; the biting sub-zero cold nights; the warm swigs of vodka; the fun-filled chatter with friends; the joyous whoops after getting the visas; the cheap flights to UK; the part-time jobs in small restaurants and departmental stores; and of course the earnings in British Pounds, the ten-fold currency conversion in the Russian black market. Yes, London was the only solution to my problem. Now I had to find my man Lenny--Lenny Mazumdar!

✣

Lenny, one year my junior, was the sole contact point for UK trips for Rostov's entire Indian student community. His father was Indian while his mother was British. Lenny's parents' love story began in a Kolkata hospital. Dr Gauriprasanna Mazumdar and Nursing-In-Charge, Sue Barker, had overcome their cultural differences and family resistance to get married. Soon they had Lenny. The young family was happily living together when tragedy struck. Dr Mazumdar died in a car accident and Sue was left to fend for the then five year-old Lenny and herself. She returned to UK and continued her nursing career. She doted on Lenny and made sure that he followed in his father's footsteps. Thankfully her dream came true when Lenny got a chance to study medicine in Russia. Over the years, many things had changed in and around her but one thing had not--she was still Mrs Sue Mazumdar and she still had a soft corner for everything Indian.

I met her for the first time when she came to visit Lenny in Rostov. With her helpful and outgoing nature, she had been an instant hit amongst us. We called her Mazumdar-aunty. As sweet as her Bengali delicacies (which she had mastered in her Kolkata years!) was her generous offer to host any Indian medical student in her London home, free of cost, till he found a job! At that time I had had no idea that I would be vying for it someday!

Lenny was as gracious as his mother. He knew of my situation and when I asked, without subjecting me to any interrogation, he simply called up his mother and made arrangements. Once again, I was going to go through the same visa and air travel routine but this time around it would be different. No friends, no fun, no excitement, just dark doubts about the future!

✣

As I walked out of Heathrow airport, I saw Mazumdar-aunty waving at me. She greeted me warmly and we started walking towards the car park. Aunty's constant friendly chatter helped to break the ice and I began to feel at ease.

"We stay at Wembley. It is a gated complex. Nothing fancy but a safe and functional 2 BHK apartment. Just two more years of paying off the mortgage and then it will be mine. Lenny's room is empty and you will be staying there. After dropping you home, I will be going to the hospital. Whole of this week, I have nightshift. There will be food in the fridge, just microwave it whenever you want. The phone and the directory will be at your disposal. Go through the classifieds and keep calling people till you land a job. Of course, don't feel pressurised, you can stay here as long as you want. But Lenny has told me about your situation, so I know how important it is for you to start working. I will tell you one thing though and that there is nothing like work to ward off the blues!"

I nodded. Without saying another word, aunty suddenly thrust a £20-note in my hand. Waving off my protest, she just said, "Keep it. You will need some money."

I tried to thank her but instead embarrassed myself by starting to cry!

That night, after aunty left for the hospital, I lay awake on Lenny's bed. Full-length posters of Indian cricketers and English footballers looked down upon me from each wall. I could not feel even an ounce of the energy and enthusiasm exuded by those sportsmen. Away from my home in India, away from my college in Russia, here I was in UK, in an acquaintance's house, waiting to get a job to pay off a huge debt! What was I doing with my life?

✣

The next morning, I woke up with a start. I was drenched in sweat and my heart was racing. I had probably woken up from some nightmare but I could not remember it. The timepiece near my bed showed 8:15am. I got up and walking up to the window, pushed the curtains aside. The morning sun filtered into the room, bringing with it light, warmth, and hope. Yes, hope. For the first time in the last few days, I felt a glimmer of hope touch my soul. I was here for a reason. I was here to turn my fortune around.

My previous stints in London had taught me the basics. As soon as I picked up the newspaper, I plucked out the classifieds section. 'Waiter wanted', 'Dishwasher wanted', 'Restaurant supervisor wanted', 'Shop assistant wanted'.... Now that would be my area of expertise! With a pencil in my hand, I kept circling the relevant advertisements.

When Mazumdar-aunty walked into the flat at 9:30am, I had already been through two futile telephonic interviews and was in the midst of the third. It was for the post of 'Restaurant Assistant', a glorified term for an all-purpose restaurant worker. The Hindi-speaking voice at the other end of the telephone was unmistakably Bangladeshi. His questions were direct and to the point. My answers were short and sweet. Of course, I could not really express what I actually felt inside while answering!

"Indian restaurant mein kabhi kaam kiya hai?"

"Yes sir." (These Bangladeshis! Why did they always pass off their eateries as Indian restaurants?)

"Murgi kaatna jaanta hai?

"Yes sir." (Cutting dead chicken comes naturally to me, particularly after all those hours spent dissecting dead bodies!)

"Bhajiya fry karna aata hai?"

"Yes sir." (With my backside on a frying pan, is it too much of a task to fry fritters?)

"Safaai bhi karna padega."

"Yes sir." (I am only too eager to clean up my sh**!)

"Ok. Sunday off. *Rehna, khaana* free. £15 per week. When are you joining?"

"Hmm. I'll call you later." (Bloody asshole!)

As I hung up, Mazumdar-aunty threw me a knowing glance and in spite of my best efforts, I could not dodge that! I was lucky that she wisely decided not to pry further into my job-hunting ventures.

✣

It was on the third day that I finally struck pay-dirt. A Southall vegetarian restaurant urgently needed a young Indian supervisor. The owner was a Punjabi guy called Bobby Chaddha and thankfully the first question he asked me was about my qualification! The moment I uttered the words 'Final Year Medical student', I could sense the wheel of fortune turning the right way. The man was so impressed that he did not bother to ask any other details.

He said, "Doctor-*saab*, I am happy that I am helping you in some way. You are hired as the supervisor if you could join us tomorrow. Sunday off, £75 a week."

I tried my best to stay composed as I said, "I will also need a place to stay in Southall, as currently I am staying at a friend's house in Wembley."

Chaddha extended his generosity even further by saying, "Oh, if you don't mind you could stay in my house with my family. We have a big house; there is an extra room. You could have breakfast with us and then eat lunch and dinner at the restaurant."

I was ecstatic!

Mazumdar-aunty was very happy for me. She wished me luck, hugged me tightly, and said, "Take care, my son. Work sincerely. If you need anything, or if you don't like the job, don't hesitate to come back. This is your house too."

As I left for Southall, I fondly looked back at Lenny's house. I really felt as if I was leaving my own house!

□□□

Chaddhas

Chaddha's Veg Delights

Chaddha's Tandoori Times

With their garish yellow and red colour scheme, the twin restaurants were quite easy to spot even in the array of Indian restaurants. While walking towards them I was soaking in Southall's 'Little India' or 'Little Punjab' atmosphere. As far as I could see, I was practically surrounded by Indians, Indian aromas and Indian music, or rather by Punjabis, Punjabi aromas and Punjabi music!

Just outside the restaurants was a typically Indian rustic cot (the *chaarpai*), on which two Sardars were boisterously gossiping and sipping Lassi in tall brass glasses. It looked a scene straight out of a Hindi film.

I walked hesitantly towards them and asked, "Where can I find Mr Chaddha? Mr Bobby Chaddha?"

They must have found something extremely funny in that question because they broke into loud guffaws. Then one of them called outat the top of his voice, "Oye Chaddhe, someone is looking for you."

The next moment a six and half foot Sardarji, in his mid-forties, came out from Chaddha's Veg Delights.

"Yes?" He asked.

I mumbled, "I am Sadanand Borkar. We talked yesterday about the supervisor's job."

Instantly his face broke into a wide grin. Shaking my hand vigorously, he introduced me to the charpaai-lot.

"He is Sadanand, our new supervisor. Beware guys, don't fool around with him. He is a doctor from Russia, who has come here for a vacation job. He will be staying with us."

Turning to me, he added with a smile, "These two fat guys are my cousins Manu and Bally Chaddha! They may appear jobless but they are not. They run Tandoori Times. Welcome to Chaddha's!"

✣

The warmth of Chaddha's greetings immediately put me at ease.

"Look Sandy, may I call you Sandy? Sadanand seems too long and a bit old-fashioned."

I nodded.

"So Sandy, here is my story. Fifteen years ago I came here to work as an assistant manager in Tandoori Times. Back in India, I was wasting my life in Bhatinda--doing some sundry food-stuff business, getting drunk with friends, indulging in street fights.... My uncle advised my father to send me here. I hated it when I first came here. But look what hard work does for you. In just six years I managed to start my own restaurant, right next to my uncle's restaurant. If you are sincere, then London does make your dreams come true."

Chaddha's dreams had indeed come true. His house was a nice, single-storied bungalow with a small garden. His wife, Jagjit, a typically rotund and pleasant Punjabi lady, opened the door and greeted me effusively.

"Welcome home, doctor-*saab*. I have prepared your room. Freshen up and have some breakfast and then Jassi will drop you to the restaurant."

Jaspreet alias Jassi, Chaddhas' daughter, was standing in the hallway. With her cropped hair and crumpled t-shirt and jeans attire, she looked every inch a bored London teenager, who was unenthusiastically participating in a family ritual.

Mr Chaddha looked at her sternly, "Jassi, why can't you ever wear something decent? Is this the way you dress when guests come over? Okay, now you may go and show Sandy--I mean Sadanand--his room."

Jassi guided me to a room that was right at the top of the house. It was a small triangular room with sloping sidewalls meeting at the top. It looked like a room converted out of an attic. Although it was nicely furnished, there was hardly any space to move around without the constant fear of bumping against the walls. But who was I to complain? All this was beyond my expectations anyway. A well-paid job, a caring boss and free lodging and boarding. Where else would I get such a lucky break? It was too good to be true!

✣

Well, as they say, if something seems too good to be true, then either it is not good or not true! Within no time, I got a taste of that. As I unpacked my suitcase, Jassi kept standing in my room, eyeing me with contempt. Then she made a move towards the door but instead of going out, she bolted the door from inside.

Keeping her voice to a barely audible hiss, she said, "So, you are the joker they are now bringing home for me. Listen, I have no interest in you medical types. I had a medico boyfriend once and he was a jerk. Pop and mom think they can at least make me marry an Indian and that is why they keep getting guys like you. But let me tell you one thing very clearly--don't even bother. I am already booked!"

With that, she opened the door and left the room, leaving me speechless.

✣

As I came down for breakfast, it became clearer. Mr and Mrs Chaddha wasted no opportunity to pamper me. The table was full of Punjabi delicacies. *Chhole-bhature, aloo ke parathe, achar, dahi-bhalle, lassi*--you name the item and it was there. During breakfast, I was thoroughly interviewed about my family background, my education, and my future plans. Every possible moment was seized to impress upon me that London was the place to come to after completing my degree and in case I did, they would extend all possible support. While this was going on, Jassi just kept fiddling with her cornflakes, looking indignant. Every now and then, her mother would try and draw her into the conversation but in vain.

The mother then decided to make a bold dash and said, "You know, Jassi is our only daughter. Whatever is ours is finally hers. We are so worried about her future."

I nervously glanced at Jassi, who was looking livid, and stuffed a *dahi-bhalla* into my mouth to spare myself the ordeal of responding. I just smiled weakly.

I was already cursing my luck. I had landed in yet another hot soup!

□□□

London Dream

Bobby left for the restaurant after breakfast. But before going, he looked meaningfully at his wife and said, "I am going to the restaurant. Let Sandy rest for a while and then send him to the restaurant at 4 pm. Since he is still new to this area, let Jassi drive him there." The wife nodded gleefully!

It was 3:45 pm, when Jassi knocked on the door to take me to the restaurant. She still looked grumpy.

I seized my moment as soon as I got into the car.

"Look Jassi, I would like to make myself clear right in the beginning. At this juncture, I have no intention of falling in love or getting married. Not with you and not with anyone else. I have far too many things to take care of. I simply have no time for all this. I have come here to work and if you feel that I am conspiring with your parents, then you are dead wrong. So quit being nasty and let's be friends."

She smiled for the first time. Her face actually lit up, highlighting her good looks.

"Oh, I am so sorry. I did not mean to be rude to you but you have seen my parents and you can imagine what I have to go through day in and day out. I want to study Architecture but they want to marry me off before I go to college. To put them off I have told them that I am in love with a Paki! "

"Are you?"

"No. Are you kidding? It's just a ruse. You know us Punjabis. We don't want our daughters, or for that matter even the sons, to study much. It is 'Finish your school and get married' for daughters and 'Finish your school and get into family business' for sons! So that's why I came up with this plan. "

"Oh, so all that stuff about you being booked was all cooked up?"

Jassi smiled. Stopping the car, she said, "Here's our restaurant. Best of luck, Sandy. You are not bad!"

✣

Chaddha's Veg Delights, a mid-sized restaurant serving a mix of Punjabi and Gujarati vegetarian dishes, was not only popular amongst the Indians but also the *goras*. My work was to look after staff attendance, restaurant cleanliness, kitchen supplies, and daily cash collection accounts. Starting the day at 10 am, I would work till 2 pm. Then it would be time to go to Chaddha's place for lunch, followed by a short nap. At 4 pm I would be back to work till 10:30-11 pm. The work load was heavy as there were too many fronts to cover but I enjoyed it. It took my mind off my problems.

After a few days, though Pop and Mom Chaddha seemed to realise that things were not going as per their plan, they were not going to accept defeat so soon. They tried all the tricks in the book. Sending the two of us on sightseeing tours, to movies, to musicals.... But Jassi and I had already reached a quiet understanding. We enjoyed those outings but remained focused on our personal goals. We were just friends, nothing more.

A month had passed since I took up the job and I went to ask for my salary. Chaddha was sitting at the cash counter. As I posed the question, he looked at me. There was deep sadness in his eyes.

"Sandy, I don't know if you are not reading my thoughts or you are simply not interested in them."

I kept quiet.

"Here I am, a man worth at least a quarter million pounds, who is offering you everything and there you are, standing before me and asking for £75 a week as salary."

"Sir, I don't know what you are talking about."

"Oh, please. Don't insult my intelligence. You knew everything from the very beginning. I am now asking you bluntly. Will you marry my daughter?"

Now there was no escape. Matters had come to a head.

"No sir, I am sorry. I have too many things to do before I can even think about marriage. I like Jassi as a friend but both of us have different visions in life. Our priorities are different."

"Oh, so that's that, huh?"

"But sir, if you are willing to listen with an open mind, I have some good news for you."

"Good news?"

"Yes, and the good news is that Jassi isn't hooked up with some Paki guy. She is just a bright girl who wants to become an architect and wants her parents to understand that! She wants your support, not this constant nagging about getting married!"

For a full minute, Chaddha kept looking at me with wide eyes. Then he got up from the cash counter and hugged me tightly. With tears flowing down his cheeks, he kept saying, "Oh thank God! *Waahe Guru Daa Khalsa, Waahe Guru Dii Fateh!* Thank you Sandy, thank you!"

✣

That night we had a big party at Chaddha's place. All his Punjabi friends and relatives had come. Drinks, dance, dinner, gossip! After dinner, Chaddha stood up on the centre table. He was totally sloshed and barely able to stand straight. Holding up his glass of whisky, he began his post-dinner speech.

"Dear friends and family members, very few people here have any idea about what we are celebrating today. Let me tell you. We are celebrating Jassi's dream. My dear daughter wants to study Architecture and I am bloody well going to ensure that she becomes the best architect in London. Let me tell you, for almost a year, I had been trying to marry her off and clip her wings but now I have realised that it was a big mistake. I have realized that I should let her fly. I cannot just let age-old traditions come in the way of her dreams. *Beta* Jassi, I love you *beta*!"

The father and the daughter were hugging and crying unabashedly. The mother was shedding silent tears. Everyone was watching in stunned silence, while I smiled contentedly. With that one bold argument, I had managed to change quite a few lives, including my own! Yes, mine too. Chaddha had raised my salary to £100 a week! It was definitely the high point of my London dream! Just a month more and I would have enough in my kitty to pay off my debt.

Dreams, unfortunately, have this nasty habit of vanishing when we wake up! When I woke up the next morning, I did not know till then that that my dream was over and my next nightmare was about to begin. There was a sharp stabbing pain, which began at the base of my neck and traversed through my shoulders and upper arms. It was so bad that I could not even move from my bed. After a few futile attempts to lift myself from the bed, I decided to just lie down and wait for somebody to come.

Fortunately in view of the previous night's party, Mrs Chaddha had decided that it would be a wise move to wake me up to get ready for work. When she walked into the room and saw me writhing in pain, unable to get up, she immediately rushed down to call for help!

The whole of next month was spent in moving from one hospital to another. My life revolved around visiting doctors, endless medicines, X-rays, CT-scans, blood tests, cervical traction, physiotherapy, and the constant fear of an impending surgery. The scans had detected that there had been a recent injury at the base of my neck but I was not able to recall any such incident till...

Suddenly it came back to me.

I was walking out of the Southall railway station...civic work was going on...cement bags hung carelessly over steel bars...

the snapping sound...the momentary stinging sensation as one heavy cement bag brushed my side on its way down... casually walking away from the scene as there was no apparent injury.

Now, the same seemingly harmless accident had come back to haunt me. The Chaddhas and Mazumdar-aunty were doing their best to look after me. They were footing my hospital bills as I had no health insurance. They were taking turns to give me company at the hospital. They were saying the right words to keep me in good spirits. But all that was just making me realise what a liability I had become in their lives.

By the end of the month, I had recuperated enough to travel but was still not fit to work. Now there was no point in staying in London and being a liability. I had saved around two hundred pounds, though that was not going to be enough to pay off my dues, but at least I had something to go back to Russia with and buy some time. I decided to take to go back to Russia.

The Chaddhas and Mazumdar-aunty came to see me off at the airport. One by one they hugged me--Mazumdar-aunty, Mrs Chaddha, Mr Chaddha and finally Jassi. Surprisingly, Jassi was sobbing and in between the sobs, she kept saying, "Why are you letting him go? Pop, do something."

In just two months, I had grown so close to these people. How could I ever repay what they had done for me? With tears in my eyes, I freed myself from Jassi's hug. It was time to say good-bye!

My London dream was over!

□□□

Back to Rostov

My London dream had shattered and I was back to reality in Rostov. With a debt of $2000 and hardly $500 in my pocket, the situation was grim, but little did I know that it was to become worse.

Just as I was about to enter my hostel room, somebody tapped on my shoulder. I turned to see the hostel matron standing there. Without a smile or any greetings, she handed me two faded brown envelopes and said, "For you."

There was something about her stern expression that told me that I was supposed to read those letters right then.

I opened the first one.

"Mr Sadanand Borkar, you are hereby notified that your monthly stipend has been stopped in view of your unsatisfactory academic performance."

Then the next one.

"Mr Sadanand Borkar, you are hereby notified that your hostel accommodation facilities have been withdrawn in view of your unsatisfactory academic performance. You are requested to arrange your own accommodation within the next 72 hours."

My mind was already busy analysing the dire situation. Losing the stipend was no big deal. As it is, with the soaring inflation, the value of those ninety rubles was practically nothing. But losing the hostel was a big blow.

The matron, however, was in no mood to wait for me to come up with a solution. She wasted no time in coming to the point.

"These letters have been lying with me for the last two months. There are students in the waiting list for the hostel. When will you vacate your room?"

"Umm...I am just back from London, Ma'am. I have not been well. Please give me a few days to arrange alternative accommodation."

"OK, you have three days to do that." And she was gone!

It was 11am. The hostel was eerily still and quiet. Everyone was attending classes. I opened the door. It was clear that two new students had already come to occupy my roommates' beds. My bed and things had been left undisturbed. I sat on the bed, clutching my head, which was feeling heavier by the minute.

Necessity is the mother of invention, they say. For me, necessity had often been the mother of lies or rather lies to mother. I had often lied to my mother--sometimes to escape punishment, sometimes to preserve self-image, and sometimes to keep my family happy. Now, I was going to lie to her once again--just to keep myself afloat!

I started writing a letter.

"Dear Mom,

My training programme in London went off well. I am sorry that I could not write earlier, as I was very busy there. Now I have returned to Rostov. As I had informed you in my earlier letter, my medical course has been extended by another year as I have decided to do a short specialisation course in Surgery.

You know how the conditions have changed here since the fall of Communism. Now the college authorities have asked us to pay $1000 as course fees. It would be great if you could please arrange the money within the next 10 days.

I hope everything is well over there. Love to you all.

Yours,

Sada

Writing the letter made me feel slightly better. I kept trying to convince myself that there was nothing wrong in not telling them that I had failed...that there was nothing wrong in asking them for money...after all, what are parents for?

Now I could buy some time by paying $500 to Sasha and then I could find a place for myself with the money that would surely be sent by my loving parents!

A soft knock on the door snapped me out of my reverie.

□□□

The Saviour

As soon as I opened the door, a tall, bald guy nonchalantly pushed me aside to come inside the room. He settled down comfortably on my bed and eyed the room with an intense gaze.

Flabbergasted by the sudden intrusion, I asked sharply, "Hey buddy, what's happening? Who are you?"

He did not reply; he just smiled--an angelic smile that felt strangely familiar. Suddenly I got it. It was Igor, my Russian roommate for six years. Two years back, the fellow had just disappeared without a trace. There had been no news of him since then. We had even speculated if he had been packed off to Siberian trenches for some anti-government activity! Igor's boozing and skirt-chasing activities had spawned many a legend on our campus and it was easy to picture him reeking of vodka, and getting caught with his pants down with some high-placed politician's wife!

"Igor? Is that you? What have you done to yourself? No beard, no moustache, no hair on your head. Are you alright? You are looking like some Hindu saint!" I burst out.

"I always thought you were very perceptive. You have guessed it right," Igor smiled.

"What are you talking about? And what is this new style of speaking? Don't tell me you are drunk at this hour?" I was getting more and more worried by the minute.

Once again Igor just smiled in response. After a prolonged deliberate pause, he finally began talking. Again there was a silly musical lilt to his speech. Every word, each syllable was uttered in a slow sing-song manner.

"Sada, I am sure you remember how I had disappeared two years ago. Well, these two years I was away discovering my own identity...who I am, what I am.... What is the purpose of my existence? So many questions had been bothering me. For months, I just wandered from place to place--moving from one relative's house to another's...and then I found out my true calling in Yalta."

"Yalta?" I asked incredulously.

"It's a beautiful city in Ukraine--situated on the Black Sea, surrounded by mountains and forests." He patiently explained.

"Ok, so?" I was still very confused.

"There I enrolled in Dharmesh Yogi's *ashram* and his teachings changed me. They totally changed me, not only on the outside but also from inside. Now I am a different person. I am not the same old Igor whom you once knew."

"Igor...Igor, what are you saying? I don't understand. You are now Dharmesh Yogi's follower?" My mind was swirling.

"Please call me his disciple. Follower sounds so clannish! In fact, now I have become a certified trainer of his holiness's teachings. I have come to work in the *ashram* at Rostov.

"Wait, what are you saying? Now Rostov has a Dharmesh Yogi *ashram*?"

"Yes, my friend. You just have to cross the bridge on Rostov River and you'd find the *ashram* right there on the South bank. I have come to invite you to work there."

My jaw dropped. I kept looking at him. Was this man sane? Or had he simply lost his marbles?

✣

I composed myself and had a good look him. Igor was right about one thing--he had indeed changed completely. The Igor I had known earlier was a handsome guy, who sported long brown hair and had a beard and a moustache to go with. His looks had often reminded me of Jesus Christ. In fact, we used to call him 'Christ'! He was a livewire, who was always cracking coarse jokes and laughing loudly.

The Igor before me was a gaunt, bald man who revelled in breaking into beatific smiles every now and then. His style of speaking was funny (without intention of course!) and the content of speech was incredible.

I drew him into a rapid-fire discussion. The first question was obvious.

"Igor, let me get this straight. You want me to work in Dharmesh Yogi's *ashram*?"

Without batting an eyelid, he replied, "Yes."

"Why?" I was as suspicious as ever.

He calmly answered. "Because I am your friend and I want to help you in your problem."

"What problem?" I snapped nervously.

"Oh, I know all about your debt and failed London trip."

For a moment, I was taken aback. Was this man, a man who had once shared the same room with me, now able to read my thoughts? Had he really picked up some supernatural spiritual powers?

His next sentence gave me the real picture. He said, "Sasha told me the whole story."

"Where did you meet Sasha?" I was genuinely curious.

He happily broke the news. "Oh, he has recently joined our movement."

"So, Sasha is also a Dharmesh Yogi disciple?" This was proving to be a conversation full of surprises.

Igor just nodded. I was getting more and more confused.

"Actually it was Sasha who suggested that I should offer this job to you," Igor added.

"So, it was Sasha who told you to hire me for Dharmesh Yogi?" I asked incredulously.

Once again, we went through the same routine. A wise nod from Igor and a look of utter confusion from me.

"And may I know why?" I tried bringing in some sarcasm.

There was no reaction on Igor's placid face. He patiently explained, "Oh, he is ashamed of his activities and associations in the past. He knows he has done you a great injustice by making that unholy deal with the Mafia-men."

"And how do you both propose to undo that?" I really wanted to know their plan of action.

Igor confidently said, "We have actually worked out the whole plan. Sasha has already paid five hundred dollars from his own funds to those men and I will be paying the rest from the *ashram* fund."

Now I was truly dumbfounded. This was something beyond my wildest dreams. Sasha paying from his pocket; Igor paying from *ashram* fund. What was really happening here? Hell, this was a bloody miracle. In a flash, my entire debt was being wiped off. Yet I still did not believe a word he was saying.

"Igor, how are you going to pay from the *ashram* fund? And why has Sasha paid for me?"

"Oh, Sada, I am now the in-charge of the *ashram*'s finances and I have full authority to help the needy. So, I am perfectly entitled to issue a cheque of $1500 to save a nice soul. And as far as Sasha goes, he is not doing it for you; he is doing it to save his own soul!"

"What work am I supposed to do at the *ashram*?"

Igor explained, "It is easy. Every evening you will be expected to work for a few hours as a translator. We only have a few spiritual trainers, who can speak Russian. Most of them speak English. So your Russian and English language skills will come in handy for us to communicate. Don't worry, we will be paying you $1500 a month for your services. So, what do you think? "

What could I possibly think? I just asked, "When should I join?"

He said, "Today."

And that was that!

I tore off the letter I had written to my mother. Igor had indeed saved my soul from getting a tad more corrupt than it already was!

□□□

Jai Guru Dev

"Igor, before I start working in the *ashram*, let me tell you one more thing. I have been asked to vacate this hostel room within the next three days." I decided to come clean.

Igor casually replied, "Oh, that should not be a problem. For the first few weeks, you could stay in the *ashram* and after that you could move into a vacant room that I have in the North Bank *Kommunalka*. Just need some time to clear my stuff."

"*Kommunalka*?" I did not know what he meant.

He explained, "It's a sort of Community Housing complex of shared apartments. In each apartment, the hall, kitchen and bathroom are common and the rest of the rooms are taken by different individuals. I am sharing my apartment with an old lady. I call her Aunt Nina. She is a widow, who shuttles between this apartment in Rostov and her son's apartment in Moscow. You could pay her $20 a month and use the entire apartment."

This was simply unbelievable. Just an hour ago, I was in a $2000 debt, without any job prospects, and about to lose the roof over my head...then enter Igor and here I was--my debt paid off, a decent well paying job and an apartment to move in! If this wasn't a miracle, what was!

"Igor, I can't tell you how much I appreciate your help. There are no words to thank you, man!"

"Don't thank me, Sada. I am just doing what Guru Dev has taught me. Okay, pack up your things. Let's get going."

With Igor's help I packed all my belongings and put it in his car. It was time to say goodbye to my hostel!

Igor was at the wheel and I was sitting quietly beside him, still wondering about his dramatic re-entry in my life. It was time to ask Igor some questions that were bothering me.

"Does Dharmesh Yogi ever visit this *ashram*?" I started with a basic query.

"No, we haven't been so fortunate but our turn will come soon. Guru Dev has currently settled in Norway, from where he visits all his *ashrams*." Igor informed.

"Why does he build all these *ashrams*?" Another basic query from me!

"Don't you see the vacuum all around us?" Igor dramatically posed a question.

"Vacuum? All around us?" Perplexed, I actually looked all around to check!

Ignoring my perplexed look, Igor calmly explained, "Yes, spiritual vacuum. All these *ashrams* are made to fill the spiritual vacuum in this world. Now take the case of Russia. For so many years, people here believed nothing but the *Communist Manifesto* and now with the collapse of Communism, they are feeling helpless and rudderless. They need someone to guide them. They need Guru Dev."

"So, are you getting a good response?" I wanted to know.

"You will soon see for yourself." Once again, he answered with a beatific smile.

"Don't get me wrong. I am just curious. What is it exactly that attracted you to this man?" Finally, I asked him the question that was bothering me the most.

Igor answered, "He is not just a man! Let's call him Guru Dev. Well, you won't understand that till you meet him. Outwardly he may not look any different from any other hermit but once he starts speaking, you will realise that he is extraordinary. His words, his thoughts...they give you a new way of looking at life. They make you feel as if you are the master of your own destiny. Why do you think people from all over the world have become his disciples?"

"But how could you just leave your medical career midway to take up this...this new way of life?" I was still skeptical.

Once again, there was that all-knowing beatific smile that made me feel small and silly. The discussion (Sorry, the 'discourse') continued.

"Sada, the important thing is to be able to sacrifice who we are for what we can become. If we remain undecided, then nothing will ever change. All we need to do is to want to achieve something great and then simply do it."

"Hmm...interesting...so is that your philosophy?"

Igor quickly clarified. "No, it is Guru Dev's. I am just following that."

Impressive! This Guru Dev was indeed impressive. Just then we reached the *ashram*.

✣

The *ashram*'s location was brilliant. Overlooking the river and surrounded by dense green woods, it was the perfect place for meditation, provided you discounted the fact that it was earlier a rather shady bed-and-breakfast motel. With its many spacious rooms and meeting halls, it was ideal for housing lots of people.

Igor first took me to their administrative office. A serious looking Black American was sitting at the desk, going through some registers.

"Jai Guru Dev."

Igor's loud greeting made him literally jump out of his seat but after seeing Igor, his face instantly lit up with a smile.

"Oh, Igor. It's you. Welcome. Welcome. Jai Guru Dev. Who is this new friend of yours?"

"Sylvester, this is Sadanand Borkar, my friend from the medical college days. He is joining us as a translator from today. Please arrange for his lodging and boarding for a month. Afterwards, he will be moving to his own apartment."

"Oh, Mr Borkar! An Indian Hindu and that too, a Brahmin! Am I right?" Sylvester asked.

I nodded. From his beaming smile it was quite clear that he was delighted to see 'an Indian Hindu and that too, a Brahmin'!

In a conspiratorial tone, he said, "It is good to have an Indian Brahmin on board. It lends a touch of authenticity to our teachings. After all, who better than a real Brahmin to explain the philosophy based on the *Vedas* and the *Bhagvad Gita*! Welcome to the FM movement! Jai Guru Dev!"

"FM movement?" Confusion was writ large on my face and Igor stepped in to explain.

"FM refers to 'Fine Meditation'. That is the unique meditation technique developed by Guru Dev and that is what we teach people. Don't worry, you will pick up the basics while translating."

My world was changing fast and I was not going to be slow to adapt. As we took Sylvester's leave, I nonchalantly waved my hand and cheerfully said, "Jai Guru Dev."

The satisfied smiles on Sylvester's and Igor's faces told me that I was on the right path!

✣

I was expecting the *ashram* to be a place full of saffron robes and tonsured heads but it was nothing like that. Most people looked perfectly normal, who wore perfectly normal clothes. They had come from various countries--Serbia, Bosnia, Bulgaria, Czechoslovakia, Poland, Israel, USA, Canada...practically half the globe was represented there. Of course, there were plenty of Russians too! A retired banker, a disenchanted lawyer, a released-from-jail gangster, a discredited politician, a reformed prostitute, a homeless widow, a jobless baker...there were people from all walks and stages of life. Together they were searching for the inner truth, finding a new meaning of life.

One just had to pay $50 as the initiation fee and then he or she could stay there as long as the person wanted. Lodging and boarding was on the house. Of course, there were rules and restrictions aplenty. You were expected to be on a totally vegetarian diet and entirely forgo tea, coffee, and alcohol. Yes, you could always substitute these stimulants with a special herbal concoction, which you could have as many times as you wanted. It was supposed to cleanse the system as opposed to the avoided items, which supposedly poisoned it!

As the days passed, I started learning more and more about the *ashram's* working. Actually it was just about following the rules; once you followed them, you were 'in'! The magic phrase 'Jai Guru Dev' was the key--with that one word, you could start a conversation with anybody and you were 'connected'. You could smile and laugh but you could not fret and frown, irrespective of the topic of conversation. All negative emotions were to be kept in check. It was supposed to be a 'happy place' and everyone strove hard to look happy! So, in a day or two, your face automatically learned to remain in a state of perpetual blissfulness! In a happy place, one could not shout or scream, so inevitably one started to speak in that soft sing-song manner!

My job was to work with the Russian disciples. The trainers would give their discourses in English and I would translate them into Russian for the Russians. Many a time I did not understand the flowery, fluffy language of those discourses but I was imaginative enough to invent some equally high-flown feel-good gibberish for my audience. The trick was to confidently motor along in a voice soft and musical! Since you could not possibly discuss the latest game scores and the hottest heroine, you had to talk about things like god, religion, truth, peace, destiny, sacrifice and virtues. After a while, I became quite adept at it.

✣

"Jai Guru Dev."

A grey-haired, pot-bellied Canadian greeted me in the hallway. From his flustered face, it was apparent that he was looking to clarify some doubts, which were bothering him.

"Sir, my name is Jim Galbraith. You are a Hindu, right? What do you think about rebirth? You call that *punarjanam* right?"

"Hmm...yes, we do call that *punarjanam*." I concurred.

"So what is your opinion on that?" He asked, hoping for further enlightenment.

Obviously I could not tell him to go die and experience the thing first hand, so I had to think. Not just think but think really hard because whatever might have been my take on that, it certainly had not surfaced in this lifetime at least. So, after trying to remember whatever little I had accidentally read or heard on this, I proceeded to give my learned opinion, "The soul is immortal. It just keeps changing bodies from one birth to another, till it finds salvation."

"Isn't that called the *moksha* or *nirvana*?" Galbraith was neck deep into this stuff!

I once again concurred. "Yes, *moksha* or *nirvana*."

With bright eyes, Galbraith told me his story. "Often in my dreams I keep seeing myself as a knight in shining armour, riding a black horse. Could it be linked to my earlier birth? Was I a knight before?"

"Hmm...it is quite possible, Jim." I acted like a wise monk.

"But sometimes in my dreams, I just see the black horse. So how should I interpret it? Is it an even earlier birth or is it going to be my next birth?" Galbraith continued to press his point.

"Jim, now that's a really interesting question. But I don't think there are any easy answers out there. The key is to make the most of what you have."

(I had learnt this particular trick from the discoursers. Whenever there was a difficult question for which you did not know the answer, you could just utter this line and appear extremely wise!)

"But then, is there an answer to my main question? How and when am I going to get *moksha*?" Galbraith persisted.

At that point, I made a strange gurgling sound and thought long and hard about sending him on an instant trip to *moksha*. It was quite an attractive option but strictly against the *ashram*'s policy of non-violence. So I decided to skip it and instead gave wisdom its due place in the sun.

So giving him an all-knowing beatific smile, I said in a mysterious tone, "That's why you are here, Jim. That is why you are here. Keep believing. What you believe will finally happen. Jai Guru Dev!"

Jim Galbraith's eyes lit up reverentially. He had just understood the deepest secret about his existence. Before he could find words for his next life-changing query, I hurriedly walked away!

✣

By the tenth day, I had had enough of this routine. That forced fake happiness, that perpetual phony philosophical air, and those clone-like ever-smiling people--everything was proving to be too much to handle. I desperately longed for some 'normal human' interactions and emotions.

Someone up there was listening to my silent pleas. Because as if on cue, someone interesting was about to enter into my life!

□□□

The new entrant

Day 11 in the *ashram*. It was 7 pm in the evening. As per the daily schedule, the *ashram* community had just finished listening to the cassette recordings of Dharmesh Yogi and his second-in-command, Dr Dilip Batra. I had dutifully played my part as the translator and as usual wondered how people could be stupid enough to be swayed by all that psycho-babble. Really, whosoever first said 'Empty vessels sound more' was a genius. These so-called discourses validated this idea everyday.

'Inner self', 'hidden talent', 'higher being', 'deeper truth', 'ultimate aim'...just empty words delivered in a 'holier than thou' manner! It also made me realise that there were enough foolish takers of this kind of crap in this world! Like so many people doing jobs they hated, I just shook my head in despair and decided to get on with it.

It was still too early for dinner, so I decided to go to my room.

On my way, was a big conference hall and it was overflowing with people. Curious to know more, I peeped in. I saw a big group of elderly Russians, standing like excited schoolchildren around a dark, stocky man in a white coat. The man was middle-aged and looked Indian. He was calling the Russians, one by one, and checking their pulse. I remembered Igor telling me that morning that an Indian Ayurvedic doctor by the name of Dr Shrivastava was going to come from Delhi to offer free checkups. So, what I was seeing there was the live demonstration of Ayurvedic *naadi-pariksha*, the technique of diagnosing ailments by merely checking the pulse.

I had nothing to do, so I decided to wait and watch the whole 'show'. As a student of allopathy, I had always been skeptical of alternative therapies like ayurveda and homeopathy. Their poor track record in terms of providing scientific proofs and their rather dubious claims of 'No side-effects' had always niggled me. So, I was rather curious to know how such doctors functioned.

An overweight Russian lady stood in front of the doctor. He carefully held her wrist, closed his eyes, and felt her pulse with deep concentration for a long time. Then he opened his eyes, looked at the lady and said, *"Aapka pet jab saaf nahi hota tab aapke pet ka vaayu mastishk mein jaake atak jaata hai. Isi liye aap ke mastishk mein dard rahta hai!"*

He spoke in chaste Hindi. How on earth were these Russians going to understand what he was saying? Just as I was wondering about this, I heard the most perfect Russian translation. In that crowd, I had totally missed out the slender Russian girl standing right behind the doctor. The same twenty-something girl was fluently translating the doctor's chaste Hindi to Russian!

The elderly Russian lady was overwhelmed by the magical diagnostic skills of the Indian herbal doctor. She just kept marvelling, "Oh, how could he diagnose just like that? He is so right. Whenever I have constipation, I have gas trouble with acidity, and then my migraine gets worse!"

Her enthusiastic response led to a fresh wave of excitement amongst the Russians. One by one, they went through the same routine. The Ayurvedic practitioner kept checking their pulse and diagnosing their ailments and the young lady kept translating his observations for them.

I had lost interest in the herbal doctor's 'magic', yet I stood there, transfixed. I was stunned by the young translator's radiant beauty and her sparkling, deep blue eyes. As she spoke in her sweet lilting voice, she kept flicking her fingers through her long golden hair. She had a perfect figure and the most amazing dimpled smile.

I was smitten. So smitten that I did not even realise when the *naadi-pariksha* session was over and everyone had dispersed!

"Mr Sadanand, do you want to get your pulse checked? Dr Shrivastava could tell you immediately whether you have the *vaat, kafa* or *pitta* disposition."

The sentence startled me. From cloud nine I had been pulled back with a thud to mother earth. I did not need anyone to check my pulse; I knew it was racing. The golden haired, blue-eyed translator was talking to me in her sweet lilting voice! Her eyes were sparkling with mischief and there was that dimpled smile on her face. There was no one besides us in that conference hall.

"H...hi, how do you know my name?" I stammered nervously.

"Not only do I know your name but also that you have been shamelessly staring at me for the last 45 minutes!" She continued confidently, still wearing that mischievous expression and obviously enjoying making me uncomfortable.

Then she decided to cut me some slack. "Oh, don't worry. I always make myself familiar with my fellow workers; the first thing I had asked the office guy was the names of the other translators. Sadanand was the only Indian name and quite hard to forget, especially in a place where one is expected to be 'always happy'! That's the meaning of your name, isn't it?"

"For a person effortlessly translating things like *Pet ka vaayu* and *Mastishk ka dard*, my name wasn't too difficult to decipher, was it?" I decided that offence was the best strategy of defense!

"Wow, that's a quick come back. I like it. I am Irina, Irina Kotova. I joined today as a translator. Nice to meet you, Sadanand." She extended her hand.

Shaking her hand firmly, I said with a smile, "Nice to meet you, too, Irina. You can call me Sada."

"So Sada, now, won't you ask me out for dinner?" Irina asked, looking straight into my eyes.

Once again I was caught unaware and found myself lost in the mischievous twinkle of her eyes. She began to laugh. It was a flowing, infectious laughter that was as bewitching as her dimpled smile.

Finally, finding my nerve and my voice, I replied, "Presently I can just take you to the *ashram's* canteen, where you can have some soup, salad, and a sandwich. As a special treat, however, I could throw in the Chef's special—a dirty-looking, green, herbal tea, guaranteed to wash away all impure thoughts out of your mind!"

"Sounds pretty interesting. The dinner date is on!"

✣

As we settled at a corner table with our sandwiches, I stole a quick glance around me. Almost every male eye in the canteen was tracking our every moment with keen interest. Normally I would have hated all that attention but somehow it made me feel good. Not just good but 'top of the world' good! I turned my attention back to Irina, who was looking at me in a studied manner.

"So Sada, tell me something about yourself. How did you end up in this god-forsaken place?"

"Oh, it is a rather long and tortuous story. Perhaps some other time!" I tried to wriggle out.

"Go on, I have all the time in the world." She persisted.

I started telling her my crazy story of failure and survival; she listened intently, hanging on to every tiny detail, never interrupting in between. The mischievous twinkle in her eyes had been replaced by a look of pure and genuine compassion. Looking into those eyes, I felt as if I could share everything with her. I went on for almost an hour before realising that I might have spoken too much.

Apologetically I said, "Irina, I am so sorry. I don't know what came over me. I have never talked so much about myself! Forget that, I have never spoken so much to anyone at one stretch."

She did not say anything. She just smiled. It was a million dollar smile--a smile that melted my heart. Then she reached out and held my hand in her hands.

Then and there, I knew it...I was head over heels in love with this girl whom I had met barely two hours earlier!

✣

As we got up, I realized that I had not asked Irina anything about herself.

"Irina, I have told you almost everything about myself. What about you? How did you land in this...what did you say earlier... yes, 'this god-forsaken place'?"

Suddenly stiffening, Irina frowned and said, "So that's the way it works, huh? Give and take? You tell me something and I tell you something?"

Her face had lost its colour. There was a strange sadness in her voice. I seemed to have inadvertently touched a raw nerve. I reached out to hold her hand but she was gone in a flash, leaving me baffled. For the life of me I could not figure out what had gone wrong in that one instant!

With a heavy heart, I came out of the canteen and started walking towards my room. The evening had turned from 'great' to 'wretched' in one moment. I had barely walked a few steps when I saw Irina standing at the end of the corridor, staring forlornly out of a French window.

I softly walked up to her and tapped her on the shoulder. She looked at me and smiled wanly. Her deep blue eyes were filled with unfathomable sadness.

Before I could say anything, she said, "Oh, Sada, I am so sorry for speaking to you like that and leaving in a huff. I should not have done that."

"Can you please tell me what exactly happened back there?"

She paused and said, "I can never tell you about my life with the same honesty and candour that you showed? Don't be fooled by my smiling face; there are some really dark secrets within! I don't know whether I would be able to share them with anyone."

She started sobbing uncontrollably. She looked sad and helpless and yet so very beautiful. I suddenly lost all perception of time and place. It was as if the world around us had ceased to exist. I did something that I had wanted to do from the instant I had first seen her. I gently took her in my arms and kissed her. There was just a brief moment of mild resistance and then she kissed me back with equal fervour!

□□□

The secret

Irina and I spent the entire night sitting in the garden. The sky was clear, the night dimly moonlit and the mood reflective. We sat there holding each other closely. Throughout the night, Irina talked and I listened.

Her sentences came slowly, interspersed by long silent pauses. It was obvious that she was finding it extremely difficult to say what she was saying and yet she seemed to want to get it off her chest. What she told me that night was an extraordinary story. It was as if she was re-visiting dark corridors of her mind, which she had locked away for years. It was not a story you could share easily.

"I spent the first five years of my life in a brothel, a plush secret place that catered to Moscow's bigwigs. My mom was one of the best looking girls working there. After meeting my father, she never entertained anyone else. They were in love but evidently he never had the guts to accept her...and me. Mom loved me a lot. When my father refused to accept me, she broke up with him. Everyone looked at her as a fount of strength but inside she was fighting a losing battle with depression. Then one day she decided to end it all by emptying her sleeping pills bottle."

"Thereon I was looked after by mom's friends. I never saw my father, never even knew his name but everyone around me said that he was a very highly placed Soviet official. He never bothered to visit me but made sure that I lived a comfortable life. Every month a tidy sum arrived in my account. I was even enrolled into the state-funded 'Gifted Child programme'. The programme rigorously trained me in everything from piano and gymnastics to ballet but took away my entire childhood. As I entered teens, I did everything that I shouldn't have. After a few meaningless affairs, I suffered a major heartbreak. I stumbled badly and had a serious brush with alcohol and drug-abuse. Luckily, a kind lady professor came to my rescue. She counselled me and turned me into a University topper and an expert linguist with command over five languages. I was working with the Foreign Ministry in Moscow till an old friend of mine requested me to take up this translator's job. Now, my only hope is to find some peace of mind."

After a long pause, she said, "Do you know Irina is a name derived from the name Irena, the Greek goddess of peace? Is this the kind of life you would associate with such a name?"

"Who says that names truly reflect the kind of lives people lead? I told you about my life. Did you find me 'always happy' there?" I countered.

She smiled. It was a sad smile, but a smile nonetheless. Then she wistfully asked, "Can anyone ever be 'always happy'?"

"Well, it should not be too difficult now that you have found me. Just never let me out of your sight and you should be alright. Let me give you another piece of advice, without even checking your pulse I can tell you that you have a *kafa prakriti* and sobbing and crying is injurious to your health. Tomorrow you could end up with pneumonia and then your ayurveda chum would have to send you to me to get an antibiotic prescription!" I teased and she smiled again. This time, it was the same old million-dollar melting-the-heart kind of smile!

□□□

Yes!

Early next morning, I was summoned to Igor's office. He looked tense and seemed to have suddenly lost his angelic Zen attitude.

"What's the matter, Igor? Is everything okay?"

It was sometime before he said, "Last night, you and Irina spent the entire night on the garden bench. Do you have anything to say about that?"

Obviously I was not going to give him a detailed account of our night out. So, wearing the same casual expression, I replied, "Nothing special. Both of us were bored and kept chatting late into the night. Is there a problem?"

He awkwardly said, "No, no problem as such. Just remember that this is an *ashram* and we don't encourage such things. You two are translators here and people look up to you to maintain certain moral codes."

"So, did somebody complain that we were doing something immoral there?" I asked, not bothering to hide my displeasure.

"No, no one complained. I saw you two out there and thought that it was my duty, as one of the administrators, to warn you." Igor mumbled. He looked weird. His gaunt features looked gaunter.

"So, have you talked to Irina about this?" I asked.

"No, not yet. But I will..." His voice trembled.

"So, I guess this meeting is over. May I leave now?" I asked, barely controlling my anger.

He must have sensed my anger. He remained quiet for a while and held out a key to me. "No, there is something else. Here is the key of the *Kommunalka* apartment. I have removed my stuff from there and even Aunt Nina has agreed to the $20 per month arrangement. So, you could very well shift out of the *ashram,* even today if you want. Of course, you can do that as per your convenience."

This sudden twist to the conversation made me search for the right words. Then I said, "Oh, Igor, er...thanks a lot. Umm... just give me a day or two to arrange my things and then I will move out."

Once again, he looked nervous. "So, you would take another day or two, huh?"

I looked at him quizzically. "Any problems, Igor?"

He hurriedly said, "No, no problem. Take your time. Just keep me informed. Well, you can carry on with your duties."

More than anything, I was puzzled by the sudden change in his demeanor.

✣

I could meet Irina only after we had finished our translation duties. It was almost 7:30 pm in the evening. The moment she spotted me, her eyes brightened. Her cheerful, mischievous expression was back.

"So, how did it go for you today?" She asked.

I replied, "Oh, the same old 'Jai Guru Dev' stuff. The 'higher being' telling us to bring out the 'inner truth' to find the 'deeper meaning of life'! What about you?"

"More or less, the same story...the same *kafa, vaat,* and *pitta* dispositions and the same migraines, acidities, and constipations. Oh, yes, there was a guy with impotence due to erectile dysfunction too; an 80-year old Bulgarian husband of a 79-year old Polish wife!"

I laughed and teased, "So, it must have been quite stimulating for you! By the way, what advice did he get from your doc?"

With mock seriousness she said, "Total abstinence for two months and a special course in deep meditation!"

We burst out laughing. A course in deep meditation for getting ready for intercourse! What an advice!

Then I asked her, "So, what was the old man's reaction?"

She smiled and said, "Oh, he actually looked quite relieved; his wife made a face!"

"I tell you, it is the women....!" I deliberately trailed off.

Irina laughed and playfully jabbed at me. "You naughty guy...!"

Her free-flowing infectious laughter was back. I just kept looking at her!

✣

After dinner was over, I broached the subject of Igor's warning. Irina looked completely taken aback.

In a surprised tone, she asked, "Did he really say all that?"

I nodded.

She said, "I never expected him to do this kind of a thing."

"Yeah, me, too. You know, he was my hostel roommate for six years. He was such a cool guy, back then. Don't know what happened to him in these last two years. By the way, do you know him from before?"

There was a brief flicker of uncertainty in her eyes and then she said, "Yes. In fact, he is the one who has invited me here to take up this job."

"Oh, so he is the 'old friend' in your story?" I asked uneasily.

She paused before saying, "Actually, he is more than that...an old friend, who once broke my heart badly."

Now it was my turn to be shocked. Igor and Irina? Where was this going?

I asked shakily, "What happened?"

She looked poised. "It was two years back. We had first met at a friend's party in Moscow. We liked each other and started going out. It went on for almost six months. I was happy that I had finally found someone with whom I could dream of sharing the rest of my life. But as always, my dream came down crashing."

"How?"

"I received a parcel in my mailbox. It had Igor's photographs with other girls. I confronted him. He accepted that he was cheating on me. He promised to change. I decided to give him another chance. Then within a month, there was another parcel with new photographs! That did it. I left him."

"So, that was the time you took to alcohol and drugs?"

She nodded.

"Any idea who had sent those parcels?"

She shook her head. My head was spinning.

Somehow getting a grip on myself, I asked, "So, what happened later?"

"After I finished my University exams, I got a letter from Igor. He had written to me how my leaving him had changed him as a person. He had written that he had renounced his old ways and found a new meaning of life. He said that now he had learned to look beyond worldly relations and had found his true calling. He told me about this *ashram* and asked me if I could join as a translator."

"Do you think he still likes you?" I asked nervously.

She remained quiet for a while, before answering. "Perhaps... who knows? But before agreeing to take up this job, I had made it very clear to him that I was accepting the offer only as an old friend. I had also written that I had moved on in life and was happy to see him move on in the right direction as well."

"So now, where do you see yourself moving on from this point?" I asked. My heart was beating wildly. What would she say next?

"Well, I had come here to find some peace to go with my name but what I found here was much more than that. I have now found a friend, who, true to his name, has promised to keep me 'always happy.' And you know what, I totally believe him!"

Even before she had finished her sentence, I took her in my arms and lifted her off the ground. Holding her airborne in my arms, I just kept swinging round and round. I was so delirious with joy. It was quite some time before I realised that a small crowd of *ashram* residents had gathered around us, who were smiling and clapping heartily. Red with embarrassment, I hurriedly brought Irina down to the ground.

After we managed to get away from those onlookers, she naughtily asked, "So, that's how you intend to keep me happy, huh?"

I winked and said, "No, that was just a teaser. Actually there are many more tricks up my sleeve!"

She smiled happily and buried herself in my arms again!

✣

Once again, we were sitting on the garden-bench. Just a day had passed in between but it had made such a big difference. Now, there was no air of uncertainty between us. We were together and we both knew that we wanted to be together forever.

"Well, I am leaving the *ashram* after two days."

"What? Why?" She reacted sharply by pushing me away.

"Don't worry. I am not leaving Rostov. I am moving into my independent apartment in the Northern Bank *Kommunalka*. Actually it is Igor who has arranged this for me." I divulged the details to put her worries to rest.

She thought for sometime and said, "Okay, I will also move in with you!"

I looked at her, surprised and thrilled by her unexpected announcement. She looked beautiful as ever. But now there was a newfound tenderness in her eyes and an air of quiet confidence. She looked sure of what she wanted. I was already sure of what I wanted. I wanted her by my side...forever!

I nodded happily. We embraced and kissed passionately. A new dawn was breaking on Rostov on Don!

□□□

Together!

Six months had passed since we had moved into the apartment and those six months had proved to be the happiest period of my life. Irina was a wonderful partner--passionate, impulsive, full of pranks and full of life. Every day (and every night!) with her was an adventure and I was enjoying it to the hilt.

In the mornings, I would go to college to attend my Surgery revision classes. By the time I came back, lunch would be ready. Irina loved to cook and she tried out new recipes and new cuisines all the time. With the menu changing every day from Russian to Mexican to Chinese to Italian to Indian, it was hard to guess what would be there for lunch. It was fun--especially since she cooked well!

In the afternoons, both of us would go to the *ashram* for our translation duties. Irina would drive us there in her secondhand but well-maintained Skoda. She was one crazy driver, always trying to challenge the speed limits and trying out unusual roads. Once we finished our duties, we would go back to the apartment. Then it would be time to explore the night. Sometimes it would be a visit to a restaurant for a candlelight dinner; sometimes a run at the disco; sometimes a movie and sometimes a long walk by the river. Then coming back home, we would hit the sack and the night would go on and on till the wee hours of the morning!

On weekends, we would drive down to Moscow and stay at Irina's apartment there. When we skipped those visits, we would have all-night music sessions. Besides being a marvellous singer, Irina was an excellent piano and guitar player. She loved Rock and Jazz and thanks to me, she had picked up smatterings of Hindi film music as well.

Domesticity had suited us well. We were enjoying living in our small dream-world together!

✣

It had taken Igor sometime but finally he had adjusted to the changed dynamics of our relations. At least once a month, he would either join us on our Moscow trip or stay with us in our apartment. His 'Jai Guru Dev' fervour had come down considerably and he was almost back to normal. The only problem he now had with Irina and me was the late night creaking of our bed!

"Will you guys ever let me sleep in peace? Are you forgetting that this happens to be my apartment? How do you expect me to continue sleeping with so much ruckus going on next door?" He would often shout from his room, in the middle of the night. Listening to his exasperated voice, Irina and I would giggle hysterically.

I would shout back, "Go back to sleep, Igor! You just have to get used to this my friend! It is a Yoga session and nothing else!"

"Yoga session, my foot!" and he would go off to sleep.

✣

It was a Saturday night. We had decided to stay in Rostov. Igor was with us that night. After having a nice musical session, we retired to our rooms.

"I loved the way Igor sang today. The last song was simply brilliant." Lying in bed, I said to Irina.

"Hmm...that was Andrey Makarevich's *Kastyor*...that's my favourite song, too. It is by a Russian Rock group called Time Machine." She said. She was looking lovely. She was also looking lost in thought.

"*Kastyor* means a 'bonfire', right?" I asked.

"Right," she continued after a while, "Do you want to know why that song sounds so touching? It is because it speaks out for every Russian. No other song would tell you more about today's Russia and its problems."

Curiosity aroused, I asked her, "Is it so? I wasn't really paying too much attention to the lyrics. What's this song about?"

She hummed a few lines and then started explaining. There was a faraway look in her eyes as she talked.

"Come wind or snow, the bonfire would keep burning through the night;

Keeping us warm; giving us light.

Still there are permissions to be secured;

Still there are questions to be answered;

Still there is red colour on the skyline.

And so much of pain to be endured.

But someone must show the courage to speak up.

For the night has been too long this time.

The fire of the bonfire may die down but its embers would still keep burning.

May God bless us all to tide over this difficult period"!

"Wow, that's so wonderfully poignant!" I expressed my admiration.

She said, "Yes, it is but you'd have to understand the deeper meaning. The song is talking about present-day Russia. The night in this song represents the hardships we are currently enduring; the red colour on the skyline means Communism and the bonfire is a metaphor for people's aspirations."

"But 'God bless us all'? Isn't that odd in this country?" I asked, curious.

"Yeah, actually when Time Machine first sang this song in the early days of Perestroika, they had used the expression 'May Destiny bless us all to tide over this difficult period.' Only after the fall of Communism, they switched the word 'Destiny' with 'God'."

We were silent for a while. We had never discussed politics before. This was totally a new side of Irina for me and it was intriguing. I pulled her towards me. Resting her head on my chest, she looked far away.

Then she asked a question to which I had no answer.

"When will we be really free, Sada? When?"

✤

"Irina, where are you? How come the door was unlocked? What's happening?" I asked. I had just returned from college. The door had not been locked from inside and Irina was nowhere to be seen. Then I noticed that our bedroom door was closed.

I knocked.

"Wait, I am changing."

"Since when have you become so shy?" I teased.

There was no reply from inside. The only sound I could hear was that of rustling clothes.

Then the door opened and Irina walked out. My jaw dropped. I just kept looking at her transfixed. Wearing a bright yellow sari with a red border, she looked stunning!

Somehow I found my tongue. "Hey, what's this? You...you are wearing a sari!"

Smiling happily, she hugged me. "Isn't it nice? Your mom has sent this. Today, I received the parcel."

My jaw dropped further. Mom? Sending a sari to Irina? Everything was a mystery. How on earth...!

Without saying anything, Irina thrust a letter in my hand. The handwriting was familiar. It was my mother's! I started reading.

"Dear Irina,

Let me say this frankly that when your letter arrived, I was first shocked and for a moment, even disappointed. We are a conservative Indian family and naturally we have always wanted a traditional Indian girl for Sada. But then as I read on, I realised how similar our thinking is. From what I have read and seen (yes, I also got your photos. They are so beautiful!), you seem to be a nice girl, who really loves my son and cares a great deal for him. What is more important is that my son is also in love with you. His happiness is of utmost importance to us and I am sure that you would keep him very happy! I have talked to his father and even he has taken quite a liking to you!

Just another month and Sada should be completing his medical education. Hopefully he will be coming back to India after that and now we expect him to bring you along! We have already started making plans for your marriage.

As a sign of our love and acceptance, I am sending you a sari, the traditional Indian attire for the bride. It is not just any other sari, it is a family heirloom. My mother-in-law had gifted it to me. Now it is my turn to give it to you!

Take care of yourself and my son!

Hoping to see you soon,

Yours lovingly,

Mother."

With teary eyes, I looked at Irina. Her eyes had also turned misty. I tightly held her to my chest and whispered into her ears, "Oh, Irina. I don't know what to say. I love you so much. This means so much to me. Sorry for not asking earlier but I am asking you now. Will you marry me?"

Looking into my eyes, she nodded happily and said, "Yes, yes, I will marry you!"

□□□

Party

"So dear, all prepared for the exam? Finally I will be able to get rid of those humongous textbooks of yours. By the way, how are we going to celebrate tomorrow? I was thinking of a small party. A nice new restaurant has come up at the Theatre Square...not too many people...just you, me, Igor, and a few friends."

Just before tucking into her blanket, Irina asked.

I had my back to Irina, so she couldn't see that I was wincing. Celebrate? I didn't even want to think about tomorrow. Every time I thought about the re-exam, I almost stopped breathing. Tension, performance-anxiety, stress...whatever it was, it was getting intolerable. I kept telling myself that I would be tested on a subject that I knew very well, but in vain. I simply could not fathom why I felt so anxious...I had never felt so tense the entire year. But that day, just a few hours before the exam, the enormity of the situation had suddenly hit me. I had started reliving every bitter moment of the previous year's surgery exam and its repercussions. It was not just another exam. It was the exam to end all exams. It was the exam, which would be making me what I had been aspiring to become.

Taking care to hide my nervousness, I said, "Irina, let me first finish my exam. Aren't we counting our chickens too early? I don't even know whether I'll pass..."

Pulling my face towards her, Irina held her hand over my lips and said, "Hey, no more negative thoughts! I know you have prepared well and will pass your exam with flying colours. So, Mr

Sadanand Borkar, quit worrying. Tomorrow is going to be a special day--from tomorrow you are going to be Dr Sadanand Borkar!"

The gods were kind. There was no Rasskazov this time around. So, there was no drama this time around. The long case of inguinal hernia; the short cases of peripheral vascular disease and cervical lymphadenitis; the theory discussion on the management of burns...the cases were straightforward, the discussion was on predictable lines and the examiners were in a good mood.

I did not even realise how time flew. Finally, after I answered Dr Olga's last question, she smiled benevolently at me and looking at Dr Andropov, a rather young, pimply co-examiner, she nodded her head in satisfaction. From the very beginning of the examination, she had been quite encouraging. It was clear that she remembered me from the previous year's Rasskazov-episode. This time, thankfully, she was the Chief Examiner.

She extended her hand and said, "Well done, Dr Sadanand! So what are your plans for post-graduation?"

Dr Sadanand? Post-graduation? Did that mean...? It seemed too good to be true.

"Yes, Dr Sadanand, you have passed the exam. In fact, you can collect your degree certificate from the dean's office tomorrow itself."

For a few seconds I was too stunned to react. Finally recovering, I muttered, "Thank you, Ma'am. Thank you so much."

After pausing for a moment, she said, "What happened to you last year was unfortunate. It shouldn't have happened. But remember one thing in life--don't let any setback upset you for long. You have to move on. Best of luck for your future!"

I was ecstatic! Coming out of the exam hall, I started jumping up and down, whooping with joy! Suddenly I saw someone standing at a distance and watching me with an amused expression. Hey, wasn't that Irina? What was she doing here?

Irina was looking at me with unabashed joy and pride. As we embraced tightly, Irina explained, "I figured you were more than a little anxious about your exam, so I have been waiting here since morning."

I never needed to tell her anything...that was my Irina. The lips locked. The world ceased to exist!

✣

The party went on till late into the night. Irina had arranged perfectly. Igor, Sergei, Kiran, Anita, Dilawar--all our close friends were there. The venue, music, dance, food, wine, cake--everything was just perfect. The mood was infectious. Everyone was congratulating me, hugging me, shaking hands with me. I felt on top of the world. I had finally been able to achieve what I had set out to...so many years ago. But hey hold on! There was something more to be achieved.

"Hey guys, I have something more to say tonight." I drew everybody's attention.

Irina looked at me, surprised.

The wine had made me delirious. I slurred as I announced, "Today is the happiest day of my life. Today I have officially become a doctor. To make this day even more special, I am going to...."

Holding Irina's hand, I said, "Here's the most beautiful girl in my life, Irina...and we will be getting married very soon!"

Applause, laughter, friendship, love...life could not be happier!

✣

We reached our apartment block just before midnight. After I parked the car, Irina hopped out and came over to my side

"Honey, I'm sorry I did not get around to telling you earlier, but I need to be in Moscow tomorrow morning. I need to leave right away."

"Moscow! Why are you going to Moscow? That too so late in the night!"

"Actually, I did not want to disturb you while you were preparing for your exam and it slipped my mind afterwards, as

I got busy with the party. I have to meet my father in Moscow. Out of the blue, he called me saying that he wants to meet me. He said that he knew everything about me and that he approved of you! Can you believe that? He *called* me. He wants to meet me. After all these years! And that too, because of *you*! Oh, how much I love you!"

Dizzy with happiness and alcohol, it took a while to sink in. "Really? That's great news. But are you going to let me sleep alone tonight? All by myself? And how are you going to go to Moscow so late?"

"Don't worry, Igor will drop me at the bus station, after dropping everyone home. Look, his car is there! I have to rush."

She kissed me goodbye and got into Igor's car.

□□□

PRESENT DAY

The photographs

The interrogating officer had sat silently, hearing me out, all this while. He had sat there impassively, minutely observing me--every facial expression, every vocal inflexion.

Now he asked, "So, you say that you came straight to your apartment after the party?"

"Yes."

"Your girlfriend left in your friend's car?"

"Yes."

"Then where is your car?"

"My car? Oh, you mean Irina's car? It must be there in the car park in front of our apartment."

"Your car is not there. Do you have any idea where it might be?"

I looked at him blankly. What was he talking about?

"How can that be? Are you sure?" I muttered uneasily.

Just then another policeman walked into the interrogation room. He whispered something into the officer's ear and handed him a thick brown envelope. The officer hurriedly left the room.

I waited impatiently.

He returned 10 minutes later.

In a strangely subdued voice, he asked, "Just tell me one thing--why did you have to kill?"

My throat dried up and my knees felt weak. It was that nasty sinking feeling once again.

Hoarsely I asked, "Killed whom? What are you talking about? I've told you so many times--I haven't killed anyone."

The officer did not say a word. He kept the envelope on the table and left the room. While closing the door, he said, "Open that packet and see for yourself!"

Trembling, I opened the envelope. There were about 15 photographs--all close-up shots, each gorier than the last. The kind of photographs they show in a Hollywood serial killer movie. Deep gashes on the abdomen, neck, and thighs. Even after seeing all the photographs, I was not sure what I was seeing or rather what I was supposed to see. I just left them on the table and sat there wondering where all this was heading.

The officer returned after 10 minutes.

He looked more composed. He asked, "So, do you remember anything now?"

Frustrated by the absurdity of the situation, I lost my cool.

"What the hell should I remember? I have told you so many times...I passed my final exam; I became a doctor; my fiancé threw me a party; I returned home and slept...and then I was arrested in the middle of the night. Now you are accusing me of killing someone and asking me to identify these gory photographs. Is this some kind of a sick game? Do I have any rights here or not?"

My outburst failed to move him. The officer's expression remained impassive as ever.

Then he pulled out two more photographs from his overcoat pocket and placed them on the table before me. These photos had been taken from a distance, thereby offering me a look at the whole body. It was a nude, lifeless body of a tall, fair girl with golden hair. Just like the rest of her body, her face had multiple deep gashes, making identification impossible.

Clueless, I looked back at the officer, still unsure of what I was supposed to do.

Then he took out another photograph. "Perhaps now you will remember...this is the dress this girl was wearing when she was killed."

One look at the photograph and I sank to the floor.

It showed a soiled, blood-stained, and an almost shredded piece of apparel. But I knew it well. It had once been a bright yellow silk sari with a red border!

□□□

The murderer

For a long time I just sat on the floor, clutching my head. I felt like howling, I felt like wailing but I couldn't. I was numb.

All this while I had kept pushing that unnamed dread to some dark corner of my mind. All this while I had kept denying that ugly thought, which had troubled me from the very beginning of this ordeal. But now, there was no scope for denial or escape.

It *was* Irina. My worst fears had come true.

Tears welled up in my eyes. There seemed to be a huge lump in my throat. I looked at the officer. His sternness had toned down. He offered me a hand to get up. I got up and slumped into the chair.

How could this be? How could I come to terms with this earth-shattering reality? In my mind, I could still see her so clearly--smiling happily, waving me goodbye. I could still feel the warmth of her body, the softness of her lips...and now I was supposed to believe that she was dead...that she had been murdered in cold blood and now, riddled with multiple stab wounds, she was lying in some cold storage.

I asked, "How...how did this happen?"

The officer looked at me intently, as he weighed his options about how much to divulge. Finally, he said, "At 3 am, Rostov police headquarters received a call from a public booth. The caller informed that a girl had been murdered and gave your address."

"But...but...where did you find...her?"

"In her car."

"In her car? But you said that her car wasn't there in front of our apartment."

"We found it in the nearby woods."

"But how could that happen? She was going to Moscow by bus. She left for the bus station in Igor's car. Where is he? Is he alright?"

The officer sighed. He got up slowly and said, "Come, let us meet him. He is waiting to meet you. He is the one who had called up the police and told us that you had killed her. "

"What?" I was startled. I looked at the officer searchingly.

He was dead serious.

✣

The officer led me through a long corridor. We came to a room, which was an exact replica of the room where I had been held up. Someone was sitting on a chair, with his back to the door. The bald head was an instant giveaway.

"Igor, look who has come to meet you? Your best friend, won't you greet him?"

The officer's tone seemed to be deliberately provocative, almost as if he knew Igor and was mocking him. The result was immediate. Igor violently turned back to look at us. He looked at me with utter contempt and hatred.

"Bloody bastard! How dare he call himself my best friend? He killed Irina. Cut her to pieces." He hissed under his breath.

I was too shocked to react. What the hell was he saying? Was he drunk? Or did he really believe that it was I who had killed Irina?

Shaken, I could just mumble feebly, "What are you saying, man?"

The officer suddenly stiffened. Pulling Igor by his collar, he made him stand up and then punched him squarely in the face. Standing just a few feet apart, even I could feel the full force of that punch. Igor's lower lip split almost instantly and blood oozed out but he stood motionless, as if he had not felt anything. The officer then stepped forward and gave him a tight slap. Once again, it was a viciously forceful slap. Anybody would have reeled under that assault but Igor stood firmly rooted to his spot. The only thing that told us he was alive was the venomous look in his eyes as he fixedly stared at me.

The officer shook him violently and shouted at the top of his voice, "Bastard, you killed her. It was you, wasn't it? I knew it from the very beginning. Speak up."

That did it. Like a punctured balloon, Igor slumped to the floor--all his venom gone, all his energy sapped. Squatting there, he sobbed uncontrollably. He started shouting hysterically, "Yes, I killed her. But I killed her because of him—Sadanand Borkar. He is the cause of all this."

Now it was my turn to slump to the floor! I just could not take it anymore!

□□□

The Confession

Almost 20 minutes had passed since that startling revelation. Igor and I remained slumped on the floor, neither of us had any strength to get up. Out of his hysteria, Igor now kept staring blankly into space. I kept looking at his expressionless face, trying to make sense of this senseless tragedy. The officer sat on the table and observed us with a steely gaze.

Finally, I could not contain myself. I shouted. "Why? Why did you do it, Igor? Why?"

He looked at me. Now there was no anger or malice in his eyes, just pain and sadness. Then he started to talk. His voice was steady, clear, and without any emotions.

"Remember the times when I bailed you out of your problems? I got your loan paid off, I gave you the job, I arranged your accommodation...I did not do it because I wanted something from you...I did it because you were my friend. But what did you do in return? You stole from me the one thing I loved the most--Irina!"

"But I never..." I tried to protest but Igor did not seem to hear me. He seemed to be in a trance.

"Do you know why I had left the hostel and the medical course midway? Because of Irina...she had broken up with me...that changed me forever. Till then, every girl had been just a toy...but Irina was different; she was very special. Unfortunately, I didn't realise that until I lost her, thanks to one stupid indiscretion. I still do not know who sent her those photographs to turn her against me but somebody did that on purpose and that destroyed everything for me. After losing her love, I lost my ability to be happy, my confidence, and even my willpower. To get over that heartbreak, I tried everything--alcohol, drugs, girls, everything--but nothing helped. I wandered from place to place, desperately trying to find peace."

"Then I found Guru Dev and rediscovered myself. Of course, I never really believed in those silly rituals but somehow they made me feel at peace with myself. After settling down into the *ashram* routine, I felt better. I thought I had overcome the past... but then they sent me to Rostov and slowly the old memories came back to plague me. To make peace with my past, I asked Irina to join as a translator. She was not keen to come down but I convinced her that I had changed and wanted her back as a friend. But somewhere deep down in my heart, I had hoped that I would be able to convince her to accept me back in her life...and eventually be more than just friends. I thought time would do the trick. Everything would have gone according to my plan but then you entered her life and spoiled everything."

"When you two came together, I was devastated. But my position was such that I could not express anything to anyone. I was, by then, a different Igor in everyone's eyes—someone who had found his true calling in spirituality. For a while, I even tried to convince myself that I was really that changed guy, who was beyond all worldly ties, but every time I saw you two together, I would burn with jealousy and hatred. I wanted to tear you two apart. I managed to conceal my anger and frustration quite well, but that party night I had had enough. You proposed, she accepted, and I was shattered inside."

"After the party, after she left you in front of the apartment, she came with me. After dropping the others, we headed towards the bus-station. Believe me, I was really going to drop her there... but then she...she decided to rejoice and share her joy with me! I had to listen to her go on and on about you and your future together; how she had contacted your family; how she was wearing the sari gifted to her by your mom; how she planned to meet her dad; how she planned to settle in India; how much she loved you...ugh...all so bloody hunky-dory, all so saccharine sweet! I struggled hard to maintain the façade of a 'good old friend' but suddenly something came over me."

"I stopped the car in a deserted spot and grabbed her. I told her how much I loved her and begged her not to leave me. I told her how much I hated seeing her in your arms. She was shocked and disgusted. She pushed me away, got down from the car, and started walking away. I got scared. I ran after her and stopped her. I pleaded for forgiveness. I went down on my knees and said I was sorry. I said I would never do it again. But she became aggressive and started abusing me. She said that she had always known I was a wolf in sheep's clothing, that she had always felt I was never really happy for the two of you. She said that it was the last time she would be seeing my face and that she did not want me in her life any more."

"That was it. I lost whatever self-control I had. I ran to the car and took out my fishing knife. When I confronted her with the knife, she did not flinch one bit. She stood there defiantly and said with a derisive laugh, 'So, you want to threaten me with a knife now?' Her taunt made my blood boil. That is the last thing I remember clearly. Her beautiful face was contorted in anger and contempt. Standing before her, I felt like a worthless piece of shit. After that everything became hazy. I hit her and kept stabbing her with all my might. I kept plunging the knife repeatedly, long after she had become lifeless. I even destroyed her face. If she did not want to see my face, why should I see hers?"

The officer interrupted. "What about the car?"

Igor calmly looked at him and said, "The moment I came back to my senses, I was shattered...I cried profusely...and then I remembered what had made me kill her. It was Sada. Everything had happened was only because of Sada. I wanted him to suffer. I wanted him to be punished. I found the car key in Irina's purse. I went and brought the car to the woods. Then I transferred the body...."

The officer abruptly sprung up from his seat and punched Igor right in the face. "The body, huh? Don't you dare call her that! Her name was Irina. Do you want to know who sent those photographs to her? I had sent them to her. I had always known what a scumbag you were!"

As the officer mercilessly beat up a visibly surprised Igor, realisation dawned on me. A fog lifted off my eyes.

The Closure

"Take this bastard away before I kill him. Let him rot in the solitary."

The officer barked the order. The subordinates, who till then were dutifully standing outside, scrambled into the room to hold Igor. With his bloodied nose, bruised face, and tottering legs, he looked barely alive. In spite of all that had happened, I felt a strong urge to go up to him and tell him that I would still remember him as a friend...that somehow I could understand his warped reasoning, his extreme step...Irina's love was like that! But I did not have any strength left. So I just stood there and silently watched the whole scene unfold.

The cops dragged Igor away. The door closed behind them. Once again I was left alone with the officer. He looked strangely subdued, quite different from the angry man who just a moment ago seemed ready to kill someone. He nervously lit a cigar, started puffing and pacing up and down the room, his limp becoming more and more pronounced.

I asked him, "So, are you going to tell me who you are? Or should I just make a wild guess?"

He looked at me startled. He held a finger on his lips, indicating me to keep quiet. Then he said in his gravelly voice, "Not now, I will tell you everything on the way to Moscow."

"Moscow?" Now, it was my turn to be startled.

He nodded slowly. "I knew you were innocent. I have already made arrangements. You are boarding a Bombay flight tonight."

"What? But my..."

He cut short my protest and said, "Don't worry. Everything has been arranged. Your stuff has been picked up from the apartment. It has already been placed in my car."

My mouth fell. He sympathetically patted me on my shoulder and said, "Relax."

Then fumbling for words, he asked, "Do...you...do you...want to...see her...one last time?"

His probing eyes looked at me intently.

I thought for a moment. Most people want to see their departed loved ones one last time, irrespective of what state their last remains may be in...without that final sight, they cannot come to a closure. Did I want that? In my mind, I could still see her so vividly. Irina...my dear Irina...warm...funny... ever-smiling...ravishingly beautiful...full of life...a fairy straight out of my dreams! I wanted to remember her that way. Just to convince myself that she was gone forever, I did not want to see some unrecognisable, dead, disfigured girl. No, never! That girl lying in some cold storage coffin wasn't my Irina! My Irina had gone forever, never to come back!

I wiped away my tears, held back my sobs, and defiantly shook my head in refusal.

For a moment I felt as if there was a flicker of kindness and compassion in the officer's eyes. It seemed as if he was about to hug and console me when he checked himself. Hastily turning his back towards me, he said, "Come on. We have to start for Moscow right away."

His voice was choked. It was clear that he was barely holding back his tears!

□□□

The way back

We were on our way to Moscow. The officer was driving and I was sitting next to him. There was an uneasy silence between us.

I decided to break the ice. "So, may I make a guess now?"

He seemed to have been waiting for that. He instantly said, "No need. I know that you know it by now. Yes, I am her father. The faceless, nameless, high-placed father who never had the courage to accept his daughter."

My doubts were put to rest. I looked at his face keenly. The puffiness, the perpetual scowl, the deep furrows, the coarse features--there was no way I could have ever connected him to Irina by way of looks. He had one thing in common with Irina though and that was the ability to know exactly what I was thinking, for almost immediately he said, "Don't try to match our faces. She took completely after her mom."

There was a sad smile on his face. His gravelly voice was soft and tender, as he reminisced. "Her mother was just like her. Warm, witty, strong-willed, and stunningly beautiful. She had never demanded anything from me. From the very beginning of our relationship, it was clearly understood that I would not be giving her my name. My position, my marriage, my family–I was never ready to lose all that."

There was a pause and then he muttered, "Prostitutes are okay as keeps; if you bring them home, you destroy everything."

I looked at him, startled.

With a short, cynical laugh, he continued, "No, don't worry. That is not how I think; that is how the whole world thinks and

I was not strong enough to take on the world! So, I just *kept* her. I was not ready to father a love-child when she said she was pregnant. But she refused to abort. She said I need not worry as she would never reveal the name of the father to the child. She said she would take care of the child on her own. She did as she promised. She brought up Irina on her own. She cut off all relations with me saying that she did not want a relationship with a coward! I desperately tried to win her back but in vain. Obviously, she was broken inside."

"Then, one day I received a call. She was dead. She had committed suicide. She had left a note for me where she had begged me to take care of Irina. I was on the verge of taking Irina home that day, but once again I faltered. I did not have the courage to stand up against the world. Irina's mother was right. I was a coward! So, I decided to leave my five-year-old angel to her fate. Of course, I lessened my guilt by making sure that she was given the best possible life my money and influence could buy. She was growing up in luxury, studying in the best possible institutions, getting everything except parental love. She rebelled. I tried my best to control her from a distance. But she went astray...perhaps that was her way of calling me back into her life. I, however, continued to maintain a safe distance. My other children had grown up. I did not want any complications. Luckily one of her professors finally managed to talk some sense into her and she got back on track. The day she graduated, I was there, not to embrace her, but just to celebrate from a distance."

"I kept an eye on every affair of hers in an effort to ensure that she did not lose her way. Igor was a scoundrel, a smooth-talking skirt-chaser and I made sure that Irina got out of his clutches. Getting his photos with other girls in compromising positions was way too easy. Then you came into her life. I could see that with you, she was changing for the better, looking so much happier. So, I did not intervene. Even before she could get it in her hand, I had already read your mom's letter. For the first time, I was truly happy for Irina. She deserved this happiness.

So, I finally gathered courage and called her. How thrilled she was to receive that call!"

"For both of us it was a very emotional moment. After spending many minutes, just clutching the receiver and saying hello between uncontrollable sobs, we finally managed to chat for almost half an hour. I kept apologising for having abandoned her; she revelled in telling me all about you and your family. I knew all about your party because Irina had already told me how she was going to plan it. We decided to meet in Moscow the day after your party. But that never happened! At 4in the morning, I received a call from the Rostov police headquarters. The Chief there, who is a very good friend of mine, just said, "Come here as soon as possible. It's your daughter...!"

The officer stopped speaking as his lips started quivering. I did not need to hear anymore. We sat there, looking listlessly at the unending straight road; two wounded souls feeling each other's pain, shrouded in deafening silence!

□□□

The Departure

We reached Moscow airport well ahead of time. From the moment we had walked out of the car, there had been tight salutes of the soldiers and nervous greetings from the airport officers along the way. It was abundantly clear to me that the man walking with me was someone very high up in the league—even in the post-Soviet era. With him in my company, the check-in and immigration formalities were over within minutes.

We were ushered into a special VIP lounge. The awkward silence that had reigned since his nostalgic outpouring still hung like a dark cloud around us. I decided to lighten the mood and quipped, "You must give me your business card; it may come handy in future."

"Future, huh?" he sighed. He genuinely looked sad.

I immediately realized the irony of the situation. Wasn't this my last day in this country? Why would this secretive, reticent man ever reveal his true identity to me? It was the last time we would ever be seeing each other.

Once again, we withdrew into our shells.

Then he suddenly said, "Oh, I had almost forgotten! I have something for you."

Putting his hand into his overcoat pocket, he pulled out a long, brown envelope. I wearily looked at him and asked, "What is it?"

He softly said, "Something you forgot to collect before leaving Rostov."

I opened the envelope and pulled out a thick sheet of paper.

"Dr Sadanand Borkar has successfully completed the Masters degree course in Medicine. He is hereby awarded the Doctor of Medicine degree by the Rostov University of Medical Sciences..."

I read it once and then twice, just to be sure. It was indeed my degree certificate, the paper for which I had strived so hard for the last nine years; the paper, which would tell the whole world that I had finally achieved what I had set out to do.

Yesterday, I would have been over the moon to hold that paper in my hand but today I felt absolutely nothing. No joy, no sense of achievement, just an overwhelming sense of loss and emptiness. The person who would have been the happiest was gone...far far away.

I looked blankly at the man handing me the certificate.

He quickly wiped the side of his eyes and said, "She would have been so happy and proud!"

My throat hurt. My eyes smarted. I tried hard not to break down. But it was impossible to hold back tears.

As I sobbed uncontrollably, he hugged me tight and whispered into my ear.

"Life is cruel, my son. When it gives you something, it also takes away something! Don't give up!"

I nodded.

"This is the final call for passengers travelling on the Aeroflot flight SU565 from Moscow to Bombay. Passengers please proceed to Gate No. 14."

I walked out of the lounge without another word.

Just before entering the passenger enclosure, I looked back. Through misty eyes, I tried to take in the sights one last time. It was the final goodbye. My Russian adventure was over.

Finally Dr Sadanand Borkar was going home!

□□□

Also by the same author

Lata
Voice of the Golden Era

Dr. Mandar V. Bichu

'Lata Mangeshkar' practically defines the sound of the entire Indian film industry. Her voice has no longer remained just hers; it has come to be recognized as the voice of Indian films. She has sung for so many different composers and yet has managed to capture the essence of each master's music through her songs. Through the medium of popular music, she has introduced the common man to the beauty of different ragas.

As an artiste, Lataji has set such high standards and created such a unique sound that she has become a reference point by which everything else in Indian popular music is judged.

I am sure that the book, 'Lata - Voice of the Golden Era', will be an invaluable asset for all music lovers who wish to really understand and appreciate Lataji's amazing contribution in enriching Indian popular music. It is a pioneering project, which will be recognized as the first serious critical analysis of a great singing career.

Shankar Mahadevan
(Excerpts from the Foreword)

ISBN: 978-81-7991-625-4
Master Code: 4373
Cover: Hardbound
M.R.P: Rs 2995/-

Popular Prakashan
www.popularprakashan.com

Dr. Mandar V. Bichu

Treating patients in the clinic; delivering public lectures and writing books, blogs and articles—everything fits snugly into Dr. Mandar V. Bichu's daily routine. This Sharjah-based pediatrician has made a significant niche as a prolific writer-journalist and public speaker. He already has to his credit 5 books, two websites and hundreds of internationally published articles on topics ranging from movies, medicine and music. *Moscow Masala* is his first foray into popular English fiction. You can write to him at <drmandarvb@yahoo.com.>